Dear Mar...

Wishing you a very Happy Birthday. We are so grateful for you and Max and our years of joyful friendship. You are a wonderful friend.

Enjoy!

Love
Jim & Colleen

5018-

BECAUSE of HIM

OTHER BOOKS AND AUDIO BOOKS
BY ED J. PINEGAR

Living by the Word

Your Patriarchal Blessing

Happily Ever After

Power Tools for Missionaries, Four Volumes

After Your Mission

Lengthen Your Shuffle

Series of Latter-Day Commentaries, Teachings and Commentaries, Unlocking, and Who's Who—Old Testament, New Testament, Book of Mormon, and Doctrine and Covenants

The Temple: Gaining Knowledge and Power in the House of the Lord

The Christmas Code

The Christmas List

Preparing for the Melchizedek Priesthood and My Mission

The Little Book of Gratitude

31 Days to a Better You

Fatherhood: A Calling of Love

It's Great to Be a Missionary

Living after the Manner of Happiness

BECAUSE of HIM

ED J. PINEGAR

Covenant Communications, Inc.

Published by Covenant Communications, Inc.
American Fork, Utah

Printed in China
First Printing: October 2018

25 24 23 22 21 20 19 18   10 9 8 7 6 5 4 3 2 1

ISBN: 978-1-52440-718-6

Acknowledgments

I AM GRATEFUL FOR MORONI'S admonition to ponder the goodness and mercy of the Lord through which all blessings flow . . . and my eyes were opened *Because of Him*. I express my gratitude to Ann Jamison for editorial assistance and timely recommendations. Thanks to Holt Zaugg for the stimulating questions at the end of each chapter. I am grateful for Shauna Humphreys for her suggestions in the final editing. As always, I am grateful to Samantha Millburn, my faithful editor at Covenant, for her constant encouragement and help in editing the book for publication. I am grateful for my family, who have taught me so much, and for my faithful companion, Pat, who loves the Lord with all her heart. I acknowledge the grace of God the Father and our Beloved Savior Jesus Christ in all things.

Contents

Introduction

THE REASON FOR THIS LITTLE book is to help us draw closer to the Lord and His love. Because of Him, we can be forgiven and made clean and pure. Because of Him, we can live in thanksgiving daily. Because of Him, we can become strong in our humility and meekness. Because of Him, we can have love in our lives. Because of Him, we can go about doing good. Because of Him, we have a straight and narrow way back to the presence of our Heavenly Father. Because of Him, we have a value system for life. Because of Him, we can live after the manner of happiness. Because of Him, we can have joy and life eternal. Because of Him, we can receive all that the Father has. Remember, the Lord has said, "I am the way, the truth, and the life: no man cometh unto the Father, but by me" (John 14:6). And this we must never forget because everything we receive is *Because of Him.*

In this treatise we come to see that Heavenly Father's perfect plan is centered on His Beloved Son Jesus Christ. Everything the Lord has done has been for the benefit of Heavenly Father's children. His life was ordained to bless us in every aspect of our lives. When we realize that our destiny is to return to our Father, it is because of Christ the Lord. The Lord has said, "*Come unto me*" (Matthew 11:28; emphasis added), and "*[Come] follow me*" (Matthew 4:19; emphasis added). As we accept His divine invitation and receive Him, we will do all things that He has commanded us to do because we love Him.

The Lord Jesus Christ, the Anointed One, came to do the will of the Father—to redeem all mankind from death and hell (see 2 Nephi 9:10, 19, 26). He suffered and sacrificed for all mankind that we might have eternal life if we but come unto Him (see Moroni 7:41). His infinite Atonement is the center and core of the gospel of Jesus Christ. This is why "we talk of Christ, we rejoice in Christ, we preach of Christ, we prophesy of Christ, and we write according to our prophecies, that our children may know to what source they may look for a remission of their sins" (2 Nephi 25:26). It is through Him that we are made perfect (see Moroni 10:32–33). The Lord has said, "I am come that they might have life, and that they might have it more abundantly" (John 10:10).

The Father has given His Son all power and the responsibility of creating all things as well as redeeming all things. He is the source of all our blessings because of the Father. We can find joy in the here and now within the gospel of Jesus Christ and look forward to the riches of eternal life. This does not mean there will be no adversity, no trials and tribulations and the associated heartaches and sometimes heartbreaking moments in life. The law of opposition is always in effect. The Lord will nurture us in all things (see Alma 7:11–12) as we turn to Him and receive His strength, through which we can do all things (see Alma 26:11–12). We owe everything to our Heavenly Father and His Beloved Son, who is the Savior of us all.

Paul noted that we labor more abundantly through "the grace of God which [is] with [us]" (1 Corinthians 15:10). God the Father and Christ the Savior and Redeemer both empower us to do good and to be good (see Ephesians 2:10). The Lord has shown us the way by word and deed. We need to draw upon the Lord's power, which rests in Him through the Father who gave Him all things. As we are faithful to our covenants "and keep his commandments," then He will "pour out his Spirit more abundantly upon [us]" (Mosiah 18:10).

In his parting words, Moroni reminds us that perfection and eternal life is made possible through the grace of God.

> Yea, come unto Christ, and be perfected in him, and deny yourselves of all ungodliness; and if ye shall deny yourselves of all ungodliness, and love God with all your might, mind and strength, then is his grace sufficient for you, that by his grace ye may be perfect in Christ; and if by the grace of God ye are perfect in Christ, ye can in nowise deny the power of God. And again, if ye by the grace of God are perfect in Christ, and deny not his power, then are ye sanctified in Christ by the grace of God, through the shedding of the blood of Christ, which is in the covenant of the Father unto the remission of your sins, that ye become holy, without spot. (Moroni 10:32–33)

Let us never forget that God the Father gave us His Beloved Son, and it is because of Him that we can do all things and enjoy the blessings of eternal lives.

With these eternal verities firmly entrenched in our minds, we can—with gratitude—seek to do all things that the Lord Jesus Christ has commanded us to do. In so doing, the promised blessings of eternal lives will be ours, and thus we will receive all that the Father has (see Doctrine and Covenants 84:38). Let us accept His invitation and *come unto Him, and then take up our cross and faithfully follow Him* (see Mark 10:21).

Chapter 1

Because of Him We Can Be Forgiven and Made Clean, Pure, and Perfect

THE LORD HAS PAID THE price for our redemption. "And now if Christ had not come into the world . . . there could have been no redemption" (Mosiah 16:6). Aaron taught King Lamoni's father "that there could be no redemption for mankind save it were through the death and sufferings of Christ, and the atonement of his blood" (Alma 21:9). Amulek reminds us "that the Lord surely should come to redeem his people, but that he should not come to redeem them *in their sins*, but to redeem them *from their sins*" (Helaman 5:10; emphasis added. See also Alma 11:34–37). The Lord has done His part for the redemption of all mankind, and we must do our part; otherwise, we must suffer. The Lord reminds us,

> Therefore I command you to repent—repent, lest I smite you by the rod of my mouth, and by my wrath, and by my anger and your sufferings be sore—how sore you know not, how exquisite you know not, yea, how hard to bear you know not.
>
> For behold, I, God, have suffered these things for all, that they might not suffer if they would repent;

But if they would not repent they must suffer even as I;

Which suffering caused myself, even God, the greatest of all, to tremble because of pain, and to bleed at every pore, and to suffer both body and spirit—and would that I might not drink the bitter cup, and shrink—

Nevertheless, glory be to the Father, and I partook and finished my preparations unto the children of men.

Wherefore, I command you again to repent, lest I humble you with my almighty power; and that you confess your sins, lest you suffer these punishments of which I have spoken, of which in the smallest, yea, even in the least degree you have tasted at the time I withdrew my Spirit. (Doctrine and Covenants 19:15–20)

Repentance is the great commandment in coming unto Christ. This is the doctrine preached in every generation, as father Adam learned. "Wherefore, thou shalt do all that thou doest in the name of the Son, and thou shalt repent and call upon God in the name of the Son forevermore" (Moses 5:8). The prophets throughout the Book of Mormon declared nothing save it was repentance and faith on the Lord Jesus Christ (see Mosiah 18:20; 25:22; Alma 34:15–17). Perfection is not so much about living a perfect life as it is in living a life of repentance. We offer a broken heart and a contrite spirit in the attitude of repentance every Sabbath day as we prepare to take the sacrament.

Repentance is ongoing. This does not mean that we continue in sin; rather, it means we become more righteous each and every day of our lives through the process of repenting and forsaking our sins. We must remember not to be mired down in the quicksand of guilt, but to start where we stand and move forward, believing in the cleansing power of Christ's Atonement. President Lorenzo Snow offers this encouraging insight: "We have our little follies and weaknesses; we should try to overcome them as fast as possible, and we should inculcate this feeling in the hearts of our children, . . . that they may learn to [behave] properly before Him under all circumstances. If the husband can live with his wife one day without quarreling or without treating anyone unkindly or without grieving the Spirit of God . . . he is so far perfect. Then let him try to be the same the next day. But supposing he should fail in this his next day's attempt, that is no reason why he should not succeed in doing so the third day" (*Teachings of Presidents of the Church: Lorenzo Snow* [2012], 100, 101).

The Lord has given us a great promise: "Behold, he who has repented of his sins, the same is forgiven, and I, the Lord, remember them no more. By this ye may know if a man repenteth of his sins—behold, he will confess them and forsake them" (Doctrine and Covenants 58:42–43). We all need and seek forgiveness, to feel the Lord's cleansing power. The Lord literally cleanses the repentant because of their righteousness, for He said, "The righteous shall sit down in his kingdom, to go no more out; but their garments should be made white through the blood of the Lamb" (Alma 34:36).

We are reminded of Enos's glorious experience when he tells us that his "soul hungered" as he knelt before his Maker in humility yet in "mighty prayer and supplication for [his] own soul" (Enos 1:4). This was neither a hasty nor perfunctory prayer. Enos describes it as his "wrestle which [he] had before God" (Enos 1:2), a prayer that lasted "all the day long" (Enos 1:4) and well into the night. "Yea, and when the night came I did still raise my voice high that it reached the heavens" (Enos 1:4). And we thrill with Enos as he receives a humbling yet powerful confirmation of the Lord's love and forgiveness. "And there came a voice unto me, saying:

> *The Lord literally cleanses the repentant because of their righteousness.*

Enos, thy sins are forgiven thee, and thou shalt be blessed. And I, Enos, knew that God could not lie; wherefore, my guilt was swept away. And I said: Lord, how is it done? And he said unto me: Because of thy faith in Christ, whom thou hast never before heard nor seen" (Enos 1:5–8). These precious words of Enos should bring joy to each of us as we consider our own lives. We become born again through the Atonement of Christ. We become saints of the Most High God. Enos tells of his guilt being "swept away," tender and symbolic words that remind us that guilt unto repentance is of the Lord, and that His Atonement can cleanse us, just as a broom sweeps away or removes unwanted dross.

Repentance is liberating and empowering. "Therefore, blessed are they who will repent and hearken unto the voice of the Lord their God; for these are they that shall be saved. And may God grant, in his great fulness, that men might be brought unto repentance and good works, that they might be restored unto grace for grace, according to their works" (Helaman 12:23–24).

Alma also had this cleansing, purifying, and joyful experience, which reminds us that we can all receive a witness of the power of Christ's Atonement to help us repent. We are familiar with Alma's spiritual plight as he "fell to the earth" in "great fear and amazement" (Alma 36:11) after being confronted by an angel regarding his crimes against God and His holy commandments, leading many Church members into iniquity. Alma was "racked, even with the pains of a damned soul" (Alma 36:16) and was horrified by the thought of facing God, and he wished for extinction.

> And it came to pass that as I was thus racked with torment, while I was harrowed up by the memory of my many sins, behold, *I remembered also to have heard my father prophesy unto the people concerning the coming of one Jesus Christ, a Son of God, to atone for the sins of the world.*
>
> *Now, as my mind caught hold upon this thought, I cried within my heart: O Jesus, thou Son of God, have mercy*

*on me, who am in the gall of bitterness, and am encircled
about by the everlasting chains of death.*

*And now, behold, when I thought this, I could remember my
pains no more; yea I was harrowed up by the memory of my
sins no more.*

And oh, what joy, and what marvelous light did I behold;
yea, my soul was filled with joy as exceeding as was my
pain! (Alma 36:17–20; emphasis added)

This is a breathtaking reminder that because of Him, we too can be
free from sin and can stand before Him, clean and pure. Yet the Lord
reminds us, through the words of King Benjamin, how spiritually vital
it is to

*retain in remembrance, the greatness of God, and [our] own
nothingness, and his goodness and long-suffering towards [us],
unworthy creatures, and humble [ourselves] even in the
depths of humility, calling on the name of the Lord daily,
and standing steadfastly in the faith of that which is to come,
which was spoken by the mouth of an angel. And behold, I
say unto you that if ye do this ye shall always rejoice, and be
filled with the love of God, and always retain a remission of
your sins; and ye shall grow in the knowledge and glory of
him that created you, or in the knowledge of that which is
just and true.* (Mosiah 4:11–12; emphasis added)

We must remember that our debt to the Lord is never-ending. We
cannot do enough to repay Him, because we are blessed eternally. And
because of this debt, our love and gratitude are never-ending and our
devotion is eternal. We will be exalted through His infinite Atonement
and our faithfulness after all we can do—or *notwithstanding all we can
do* (see 2 Nephi 25:23). Because of Him, we can repent and be forgiven

of our sins; we can be made clean and pure, having our "garments . . . washed white through the blood of the Lamb" (Alma 13:11).

Questions to Ponder

- In what ways can I apply Christ's Atonement in my life? (Think small daily actions.)

Chapter 2

BECAUSE OF HIM WE SEE THAT
MEEKNESS IS EMPOWERING

"CHRISTLIKE ATTRIBUTES ARE GIFTS FROM God. [These attributes] come as [we] use [our] agency righteously. . . . With a desire to please God, [we have to] recognize [our] weaknesses and be willing and anxious to improve" (*Preach My Gospel: A Guide to Missionary Service* [2004], 115). Elder Ulisses Soares of the Quorum of the Twelve Apostles states, "Meekness is vital for us to become more Christlike. Without it we won't be able to develop other important virtues. Being meek does not mean weakness, but it does mean behaving with goodness and kindness, showing strength, serenity, healthy self-worth, and self-control. Meekness was one of the most abundant attributes in the Savior's life. He Himself taught His disciples, 'Learn of me; for I am meek and lowly of heart' [Matthew 11:29]" ("Be Meek and Lowly of Heart," *Ensign* or *Liahona*, Nov. 2013).

Why was the Lord's meekness so empowering? Because in His submissiveness to the Father, He was given the power of God. "For God was with him" (Acts 10:38). Meekness engenders the power of humility, which defines our relationship with God the Father. It signals our dependence upon Him, and thus, like our Savior Jesus Christ, we are empowered by God and His grace through the power of the Holy Ghost. It is through humility that we come to know our Heavenly Father and our Savior.

Indeed, the Son knew the Father. "All things are delivered unto me of my Father: and no man knoweth the Son, but the Father; neither knoweth any man the Father, save the Son, and he to whomsoever the Son will reveal him" (Matthew 11:27). And the Lord knew the Father because He was dependent on the Father to the ultimate degree. He said, "I can of mine own self do nothing: as I hear, I judge: and my judgment is just; because I seek not mine own will, but the will of the Father which hath sent me" (John 5:30). Herein is the ultimate example of perfect humility and obedience, which was demonstrated so beautifully in the great and glorious premortal council: "Here am I, send me" (Abraham 3:27). God the Father gave the Lord Jesus Christ great power because He was meek and lowly.

Humility opens the door to the power of God.

Strength comes to the meek and lowly! In speaking to the haughty, unbelieving Pharisees, Jesus said, "When ye have lifted up the Son of man, then shall ye know that I am he, and that I do nothing of myself; but as my Father hath taught me, I speak these things. And he that sent me is with me: the Father hath not left me alone; for I do always those things that please him" (John 8:28–29). Nor will we ever be left alone when we are humble, meek, and obedient. Humility opens the door to the power of God, wherein all power resides. Moroni explains this empowerment as we come unto Christ: "And if men come unto me I will show unto them their weakness. I give unto men weakness that they may be humble; and my grace is sufficient for all men that humble themselves before me; for if they humble themselves before me, and have faith in me, then will I make weak things become strong unto them" (Ether 12:27). What a powerful promise!

The Lord exalts the attributes of a child when He says, "Verily I say unto you, Except ye be converted, and become as little children, ye shall not enter into the kingdom of heaven. Whosoever therefore shall humble himself as this little child, the same is greatest in the kingdom of heaven" (Matthew 18:3–4). Humility becomes our strength in the Lord because as His little children, we are totally dependent upon Him for our strength. Ammon was humble; therefore, he had the strength of the Lord. Ammon illustrated this principle beautifully when recounting the joy and successes of his missionary experiences among the Lamanites. "I do not boast in my own strength, nor in my own wisdom; . . . as to my strength I am weak; . . . but I will boast of my God, for in his strength I can do all things" (Alma 26:11–12).

King Benjamin taught that one "becometh a saint through the atonement of Christ the Lord, and becometh as a child, submissive, meek, humble, patient, full of love, willing to submit to all things which the Lord seeth fit to inflict upon him, even as a child doth submit to his father" (Mosiah 3:19). Alma recommended these attributes to the Saints in Gideon and to all Saints everywhere when he said, "And now I would that ye should be humble, and be submissive and gentle; easy to be entreated; full of patience and long-suffering; being temperate in all things; being diligent in keeping the commandments of God at all times; asking for whatsoever things ye stand in need, both spiritual and temporal; always returning thanks unto God for whatsoever things ye do receive" (Alma 7:23). The scriptures are clear as to the importance and power of humility, which is empowering because all power resides in the Father.

Prayer is a great example of meekness, lowliness, and humility, and is an integral form of worship. Alma quotes the words of the prophet Zenos, who humbly acknowledges Heavenly Father's mercy and kindness as He hears and answers our prayers wherever we might be, or in whatever situation we may find ourselves—be it in the wilderness, in our fields or homes, in our closets, in our congregations, or in the extremities of our afflictions and trials (see Alma 33:3–11). Our Savior was ever calling upon His Father in prayer to commune with Him. The scriptures record many such occasions. He prayed before beginning His ministry: "Then was Jesus led up of the Spirit into the wilderness to be with God" (Joseph

Smith Translation, Matthew 4:1 [see also Matthew 4:1, footnote *b*]). He prayed morning and night: "And in the morning, rising up a great while before day, he went out, and departed into a solitary place, and there prayed" (Mark 1:35); "And when he had sent them away, he departed into a mountain to pray" (Mark 6:46). He prayed before calling His Twelve Apostles: "And it came to pass in those days, that he went out into a mountain to pray, and continued all night in prayer to God. And when it was day, he called unto him his disciples: and of them he chose twelve, whom also he named apostles" (Luke 6:12–13). He prayed on the Mount of Transfiguration: "And as he prayed, the fashion of his countenance was altered, and his raiment was white and glistering. And, behold, there talked with him two men, which were Moses and Elias" (Luke 9:29–30). He prayed in the Garden of Gethsemane: "And he went a little further, and fell on his face, and prayed, saying, O my Father, if it be possible, let this cup pass from me: nevertheless not as I will, but as thou wilt" (Matthew 26:39).

The Savior exemplified every commandment He gave because of the deference He gave His Father in being obedient and humble before Him. The Lord exalted the doctrine of meekness and humility in His teachings. He said, "Blessed are the meek: for they shall inherit the earth" (Matthew 5:5). "Whosoever therefore shall humble himself as this little child, the same is greatest in the kingdom of heaven" (Matthew 18:4). And He reminds us that "whosoever exalteth himself shall be abased; and he that humbleth himself shall be exalted" (Luke 14:11).

With all these examples of humility and meekness ringing in our ears, we should seek to know Heavenly Father and our Savior Jesus Christ, for "this is life eternal" (John 17:3), *and seek to strengthen our relationship with Them because we are totally dependent upon Them*—and that is humility! The fruits of humility are being submissive, teachable, and easily entreated, giving credit to God for all things. Prayer strengthens our humility, as exemplified by the words of Mormon in the book of Helaman: "Nevertheless they did fast and pray oft, and did wax stronger and stronger in their humility, and

The Savior exemplified every commandment He gave.

firmer and firmer in the faith of Christ, unto the filling their souls with joy and consolation, yea, even to the purifying and the sanctification of their hearts, which sanctification cometh because of their yielding their hearts unto God" (Helaman 3:35). In other words, as we yield our hearts to God, we show our complete dependence upon Him and our submission to His will.

We are counseled by Peter, "Likewise, ye younger, submit yourselves unto the elder. Yea, all of you be subject one to another, and be clothed with humility: for God resisteth the proud, and giveth grace to the humble" (1 Peter 5:5). Alma reminds us, "Therefore, blessed are they who humble themselves without being compelled to be humble" (Alma 32:16). As a result of the preaching of Helaman and his brethren, "the people did humble themselves because of their words, insomuch that they were highly favored of the Lord, and thus they were free from wars and contentions among themselves, yea, even for the space of four years" (Alma 48:20).

In our best days when we are going about doing good, we should remember the words of Mormon: "But behold, that which is of God inviteth and enticeth to do good continually; wherefore, every thing which inviteth and enticeth to do good, and to love God, and to serve him, is inspired of God" (Moroni 7:13).

The very reason the Savior went about doing good was because "God was with him" (Acts 10:38). We always defer our good works and blessings to the goodness and grace of God the Father and our Lord and Savior Jesus Christ. And this is why the Lord said, "And no one can assist in this work except he shall be humble and full of love, having faith, hope, and charity, being temperate in all things, whatsoever shall be entrusted to his care" (Doctrine and Covenants 12:8). The Savior is reminding us that our motives must be pure and free from self-aggrandizement. As Elder Ulisses Soares reminds us, "It does mean behaving with goodness and kindness"

("Be Meek and Lowly of Heart," *Ensign* or *Liahona*, Nov. 2013). We achieve this only through God's power.

How do we call upon the power of God? What does He require of us to empower us to do His will and go about doing good? We ask! The Lord has said, "Ask, and ye shall receive; knock, and it shall be opened unto you" (Doctrine and Covenants 4:7). Asking for help is a demonstration of our meekness and humility. This is what started the great and marvelous Restoration. Young Joseph read, "If any of you lack wisdom, let him ask of God, that giveth to all men liberally, and upbraideth not" (James 1:5). Joseph's response demonstrates his meekness and humility, his willingness to trust God's promise of spiritual power: "Never did any passage of scripture come with more power to the heart of man than this did at this time to mine. It seemed to enter with great force into every feeling of my heart. I reflected on it again and again, knowing that if any person needed wisdom from God, I did; for how to act I did not know, and unless I could get more wisdom than I had, I would never know; for the teachers of religion of the different sects understood the same passages of scripture so differently as to destroy all confidence in settling the question by an appeal to the Bible" (Joseph Smith—History 1:12). And thus, the windows of heaven were opened, and Joseph saw the Father and the Son. Asking of God and trusting—as did Joseph— that He will answer our prayers demonstrate our meekness and humility.

Remember, the grace of God is always sufficient and available to the meek and lowly: "My grace is sufficient for the meek" (Ether 12:26). Alma described meekness when he said,

> But that ye would humble yourselves before the Lord, and call on his holy name, and watch and pray continually, that ye may not be tempted above that which ye can bear, and thus be led by the Holy Spirit, becoming humble, meek, submissive, patient, full of love and all long-suffering; having faith on the Lord; having a hope

that ye shall receive eternal life; having the love of God always in your hearts, that ye may be lifted up at the last day and enter into his rest. (Alma 13:28–29)

And consider the bounteous blessings of the Savior's grace as we humbly repent; they are incremental and empowering: "And the remission of sins bringeth *meekness,* and lowliness of heart; *and because of meekness* and lowliness of heart *cometh the visitation of the Holy Ghost, which Comforter filleth with hope and perfect love, which love endureth by diligence unto prayer, until the end shall come when all the saints shall dwell with God"* (Moroni 8:26; emphasis added). The blessings of the Holy Ghost are empowering.

Yes, the Lord reminds us of the foundational power of meekness when He said, "Learn of me, and listen to my words; walk in the meekness of my Spirit, and you shall have peace in me" (Doctrine and Covenants 19:23); and later on He said, "No power or influence can or ought to be maintained by virtue of the priesthood, only by persuasion, by long-suffering, *by gentleness and meekness,* and by love unfeigned" (Doctrine and Covenants 121:41; emphasis added). Meekness and humility are the underlying virtues of all spiritual growth. Elder Soares admonishes us, "We are blessed to be born with the seed of meekness in our hearts. We need to understand that it is not possible to grow and develop that seed in the twinkling of an eye but rather through the process of time. Christ asks us to 'take up our cross daily' [Luke 9:23], meaning that it must be [our] constant focus and desire" (Soares, "Be Meek and Lowly of Heart").

Questions to Ponder

- How are meekness and humility manifest in my life?

- In what ways can I "yield my heart to God"?

Chapter 3

Because of Him We Can Have Grateful Hearts

Moroni has exhorted us to ponder the mercy of the Lord from the time of Adam down to the present (see Moroni 10:3). Why? So we could be drawn to the Lord through gratitude for all that He has done. When we recognize all the tender mercies and goodness given to us by the Lord, our hearts will be changed forever. The Lord sought to draw us to Him through His great suffering and sacrifice, which made His Atonement possible (see 3 Nephi 27:13–14). Worshipping with the sacrificial offerings of the firstlings of their flocks from the time of Adam down to Christ was to point the people to Christ through gratitude for His infinite Atonement, "a similitude of the sacrifice of the Only Begotten of the Father" (Moses 5:7).

In addition, the Lord has commanded us to acknowledge His hand in all things (see Doctrine and Covenants 59:21). Amulek reminds us, "Humble yourselves even to the dust, and worship God, in whatsoever place ye may be in, in spirit and in truth; *and that ye live in thanksgiving daily, for the many mercies and blessings which he doth bestow upon you*" (Alma 34:38; emphasis added). Elder James E. Talmage once observed that "God requires thanksgiving, praise and worship, not for His gratification as the recipient of adulation, but for the good of His children" (*Sunday Night Talks by Radio,* 2d ed. [Salt Lake City: The Church of

Jesus Christ of Latter-day Saints, 1931], 486). The good we receive by developing a grateful heart is immeasurable. It cultivates feelings of reverence for God and, thereby, opens our souls to the influence of the Holy Spirit. It allows us to find joy in the here and now. A thankful heart allows us to face trials, firm in the knowledge of our Heavenly Father's love for us.

The Lord gave thanks as He administered the sacrament (see Matthew 26:27–28; Luke 22:19; 1 Corinthians 11:24). He gave thanks before feeding the five thousand (see John 6:11). He gave thanks prior to raising Lazarus from the dead (see John 11:41). We can follow the example of our Savior as we take the counsel of President Howard W. Hunter: *"Gratitude is a spiritual attribute.* One of the most esteemed spiritual attributes we can acquire in life is sincere gratitude. It enriches our lives as we, through this attribute, enrich the lives of others. If we have a thankful heart we will have the blessings that come from constant appreciation for the things done for us and the Lord's goodness. . . . Happiness and joy from blessings are never complete until there is a deep feeling of gratitude within oneself which moves an expression of appreciation" (Clyde J. Williams, ed., *The Teachings of Howard W. Hunter* [Salt Lake City: Bookcraft, 1997], 92–93).

> *Gratitude is not simply a suggestion from the Lord; it is a supreme commandment.*

Gratitude is not simply a suggestion from the Lord; it is a supreme commandment, the violation of which offends God. "And in nothing doth man offend God . . . save those who confess not his hand in all things" (Doctrine and Covenants 59:21). We should follow the Lord's commandment and thank Heavenly Father in all things (see Doctrine and Covenants 59:7). We should follow Amulek's counsel and pray over all things and "live in thanksgiving daily" (Alma 34:38). President Ezra

Taft Benson reminds us, "The Prophet Joseph said at one time that one of the greatest sins of which the Latter-day Saints would be guilty is the sin of ingratitude. I presume most of us have not thought of that as a great sin. There is a great tendency for us in our prayers and in our pleadings with the Lord to ask for additional blessings. But sometimes I feel we need to devote more of our prayers to expressions of gratitude and thanksgiving for blessings already received" (*God, Family, Country: Our Three Great Loyalties* [Salt Lake City: Deseret Book, 1974], 199).

If ingratitude is considered one of the greatest sins, then gratitude must be one of the greatest virtues. And it is! It is the precursor to love—the great commandment—and fuels our desire to change. Cicero said, "A thankful heart is not only the greatest virtue, but the parent of all other virtues" (*The Book of Positive Quotations*, arranged by John Cook, 2nd ed. [Minneapolis: Fairview Press, 1993], 78).

Once the seed of gratitude is nurtured within our hearts, we are changed forever because a grateful heart is connected by the power of the Holy Spirit to the mind and will of God. Miraculous! We feel different! We act differently! *And we are different*! It is part of being born again because gratitude is the catalyst of the mighty change.

Practice expressing gratitude. Count your many blessings. Look for the good when good is hard to find.

Remember, because of Him, gratitude can turn . . .

adversity into opportunity.

discouragement into hope.

envy into charity.

sorrow into joy.

jealousy into love.

an enemy into a friend.

weakness into strength.

restlessness into peace.

doubt into faith.

helplessness into prayer.

trials into blessings.
hatred into love.
pride into humility.
greed into generosity.
selfishness into caring.

A grateful heart can empower us to make the mighty change through the goodness and mercy of God.

Questions to Ponder

- How can I better express my gratitude for the tender mercies God has shown me?

Chapter 4

BECAUSE OF HIM WE CAN BE LOVING

LOVE IS THE SUPREME COMMANDMENT, and the law is fulfilled within the power and expression of love. When asked by a Pharisee, "Master, which is the great commandment in the law? Jesus said unto him, Thou shalt love the Lord thy God with all thy heart, and with all thy soul, and with all thy mind. This is the first and great commandment. And the second is like unto it, Thou shalt love thy neighbour as thyself. On these two commandments hang all the law (the five books of Moses) and the prophets (all the prophets' writings in the Old Testament)" (Matthew 22:36–40; parentheses added). Love is the supreme act of goodness and the motivation for all that is righteous.

John reminds us, "He that loveth not knoweth not God; for God is love" (1 John 4:8). And what is this love that we speak so much about? It is compassion and concern that moves us to action. It is found within the very attributes of the Father and the Son. It is the very nature of Their beings, as the scriptures testify. "For God so loved the world, that he gave his only begotten Son, that whosoever believeth in him should not perish, but have everlasting life" (John 3:16). "[Christ] doeth not anything save it be for the benefit of the world; for he loveth the world, even that he layeth down his own life that he may draw all men unto him. Wherefore, he commandeth none that they shall not partake of his salvation" (2 Nephi 26:24). Because of Their great example of love, we too should love. "Beloved, let us love one another: for love is of God; and every one that loveth is born of God, and knoweth God. He that loveth not knoweth not God; for God is love" (1 John 4:7–8). When we lack love, life becomes difficult in every way because we are estranged from God and our fellowmen.

How do we receive Their love? When we accept the goodness and grace of Heavenly Father and our Savior Jesus Christ into our very being, we become new creatures. We receive all the ordinances and covenants within the gospel of Jesus Christ. We make covenants and commitments with the Father and the Son. We come unto Christ and we seek to do the will of our Heavenly Father. We joy in showing our love through obedience to Their commandments. The Savior clearly states the direct correlation between love and obedience. "If ye love me, keep my commandments" (John 14:15). "He that hath my commandments, and keepeth them, he it is that loveth me" (John 14:21).

We joy in showing our love for others as we serve them, for indeed we are serving God when we do so. King Benjamin, that mighty Book of Mormon prophet-king, reminds us that "when [we] are in the service of [our] fellow beings [we] are only in the service of [our] God" (Mosiah 2:17). And the Savior's words confirm this principle. "Verily I say unto you, Inasmuch as ye have done it unto one of the least of these my brethren, ye have done it unto me" (Matthew 25:40). We are reminded of the tender words in the hymn "A Poor Wayfaring Man of Grief" sung prior to the martyrdom of the Prophet Joseph Smith. The hymn builds from verse to verse, telling of various encounters with a stranger who is hungry, thirsty, cold and homeless, wounded, and, finally, condemned to die. In each case the narrator gives aid and comfort, even offering to die in the condemned man's place. We thrill at the climactic and breathtaking final verse: "Then in a moment to my view / The stranger started from disguise. / The tokens in his hands I knew; / The Savior stood before mine eyes. / He spake, and my poor name he named, / 'Of

Charity . . . gives us new eyes to see, hearts to feel compassion and concern for everyone.

me thou hast not been ashamed. / These deeds shall thy memorial be; / Fear not, thou didst them unto me'" (*Hymns*, no. 29). We pray unto the Father with all the energy of our hearts, that we may be filled with the pure love of Christ, "which he hath bestowed upon all who are true followers of his Son, Jesus Christ; that [we] may become the sons [and daughters] of God" (Moroni 7:48). The answers to our prayers become different as we rise in the morning, and thoughts stir within our minds and prick our hearts with gentle reminders, "Who can I bless?"; "Where can I serve?"; "Who needs a helping hand or an encouraging word?" Charity, with all its trailing blessings and power, gives us new eyes to see, hearts to feel compassion and concern for everyone, and the strength to do something for their eternal welfare . . . one small deed at a time. Loving-kindness becomes the radiance and aura of our very being. We become even as He is (see 3 Nephi 27:27). We find joy in going about doing good. Peter has taught,

> Grace and peace be multiplied unto you through the knowledge of God, and of Jesus our Lord,
>
> According as his divine power hath given unto us all things that pertain unto life and godliness, through the knowledge of him that hath called us to glory and virtue:
>
> Whereby are given unto us exceeding great and precious promises: that by these ye might be partakers of the divine nature, having escaped the corruption that is in the world through lust.

And beside this, giving all diligence, add to your faith virtue; and to virtue knowledge;

And to knowledge temperance; and to temperance patience; and to patience godliness;

And to godliness brotherly kindness; and to brotherly kindness charity.

For if these things be in you, and abound, they make you that ye shall neither be barren nor unfruitful in the knowledge of our Lord Jesus Christ.

But he that lacketh these things is blind, and cannot see afar off, and hath forgotten that he was purged from his old sins.

Wherefore the rather, brethren, give diligence to make your calling and election sure: for if ye do these things, ye shall never fall. (2 Peter 1:2–10)

These supernal verses carry the knowledge and power of receiving the pure love of Christ and His divine nature. They help us in our becoming full of charity. Charity is required to come into the presence of God the Father and our Savior . . . because we become like Them. Mormon reminds us, "When he shall appear we shall be like him, for we shall see him as he is; that we may have this hope; that we may be purified even as he is pure. Amen" (Moroni 7:48).

Love is not only the pure motive of all that is good—it becomes the power within us to do good. It makes us what we are. This is why we pray with all the energy of heart to receive the pure love of Christ. This is why we give all diligence to becoming full of charity (see 2 Peter 1:7). Indeed, we should earnestly strive to cultivate charity—to love purely as Christ loves—and our lives will be filled with happiness and joy. Remember the purpose and power of the fruit of the tree of life. "I beheld a tree, whose fruit (the love of God) was desirable to make one happy" (1 Nephi 8:10; parentheses added). Yes, everything the Father and the Son do is for our happiness and joy. The Lord reminds us,

> As the Father hath loved me, so have I loved you: continue ye in my love.
>
> If ye keep my commandments, ye shall abide in my love; even as I have kept my Father's commandments, and abide in his love.
>
> These things have I spoken unto you, that my joy might remain in you, and that your joy might be full.
>
> This is my commandment, That ye love one another, as I have loved you.
>
> Greater love hath no man than this, that a man lay down his life for his friends.
>
> Ye are my friends, if ye do whatsoever I command you.
>
> Henceforth I call you not servants; for the servant knoweth not what his lord doeth: but I have called you friends; for all things that I have heard of my Father I have made known unto you. (John 15:9–15)

We become the friends of Christ as we keep His commandments, paramount among which is His commandment to love one another.

The family of God, every living soul on this earth, is the work of the Father and the Son. We love and live for our own families too. Is this enough? The Prophet Joseph taught a transcending truth that gives us the vision and expanse of love: "Love is one of the chief characteristics of Deity, and ought to be manifested by those who aspire to be the sons of God. A man filled with the love of God, is not content with blessing his family alone, but ranges through the whole world, anxious to bless the whole human race" (*Teachings of Presidents of the Church: Joseph Smith* [2011], ch. 37). Our love needs to be expressed to all of God's children.

The Savior reinforced this truth in the parable of the Good Samaritan. Yes, everyone is a child of God. And we are commanded to love everyone. The Lord has said, "A new commandment I give unto you, That ye love one another; as I have loved you, that ye also love one another. By this shall all men know that ye are my disciples, if ye have love one to another" (John 13:34–35). When we truly believe this, we will be different. We will change. We will be the Lord's disciples, loving each other and seeking to feed His sheep.

To express love is the greatest joy of the human soul.

To be loved is the greatest need of the human soul. To express love is the greatest joy of the human soul. Yes, love fulfills all the laws and the prophets. Love is the very motive behind every commandment, doctrine, and blessing from the Lord. Loving-kindness is the very expression of the gentleness and goodness of our Savior and His perfect life. Remember, He has commanded us to become like Him. "Therefore, what manner of men [and women] ought ye to be? Verily I say unto you, even as I am" (3 Nephi 27:27). And He has the power to perfect us to become even as He is.

Questions to Ponder

- Who needs my love today, and how will I show it?

Chapter 5

BECAUSE OF HIM WE WERE ORDAINED TO DO GOOD

THROUGH THE GRACE OF GOD the Father and the Savior Jesus Christ, we were ordained to do good. "For we are his workmanship, *created in Christ Jesus unto good works*, which God hath before ordained that we should walk in them" (Ephesians 2:10; emphasis added). Paul continued his teaching on doing good when he said, "I can do all things through Christ which strengtheneth me" (Philippians 4:13).

Faith, hope, and charity qualify us for the work of the Lord with "an eye single to the glory of God" (Doctrine and Covenants 4:5). These qualities reside in the Lord, and Alma was inspired to say, "And see that ye have faith, hope, and charity, and then ye will always abound in good works" (Alma 7:24). We can do good works because we exercise faith in Christ, who has the power to do all things (see 1 Nephi 7:12), and our hope in Christ comes by faith and is an anchor to our souls (see Ether 12:4), and charity is the pure love of Christ, which never fails, and is the motive of all righteousness, which the Father bestows upon all the true followers of His Son (see Moroni 7:48). "For it is God which worketh in you both to will and to do of his good pleasure" (Philippians 2:13).

And thus was the Lord Himself blessed through the Father. "How God anointed Jesus of Nazareth with the Holy Ghost and with power:

who went about doing good, and healing all that were oppressed of the devil; *for God was with him*" (Acts 10:38; emphasis added). God is with us by the power of the Holy Ghost, which He has given us. "Father, thou hast given them the Holy Ghost because they believe in me; and thou seest that they believe in me because thou hearest them, and they pray unto me; and they pray unto me because I am with them" (3 Nephi 19:22).

The Lord counsels us, "And now, verily, verily, I say unto thee, put your trust in that Spirit which leadeth to do good—yea, to do justly, to walk humbly, to judge righteously; and this is my Spirit. Verily, verily, I say unto you, I will impart unto you of my Spirit, which shall enlighten your mind, which shall fill your soul with joy; and then shall ye know, or by this shall you know, all things whatsoever you desire of me, which are pertaining unto things of righteousness, in faith believing in me that you shall receive" (Doctrine and Covenants 11:12–14). As disciples of the Lord, we will follow Him and seek to do the will of the Father and do all things that please Him (see Matthew 12:50; John 8:29).

> *Being good usually entails blessing another's life.*

We must never forget that we have the power to do good and to bear fruit, so long as we are connected to Christ. He is the vine; we are the branches. "Now ye are clean through the word which I have spoken unto you. Abide in me, and I in you. As the branch cannot bear fruit of itself, except it abide in the vine; no more can ye, except ye abide in me. I am the vine, ye are the branches: He that abideth in me, and I in him, the same bringeth forth much fruit: for without me ye can do nothing" (John 15:3–5).

Saints of the Most High God go about doing good. What a choice admonition and calling! What is good? All good comes from God (see Moroni 7:12). Goodness is righteousness. Being good usually entails blessing another's life. Good is that which is morally right. Goodness is godliness. Goodness and mercy are attributes of God. Doing good is the essence of mortality. Doing good keeps us on the path to eternal life. This is why faith, hope, and charity always result in good works (see Alma 7:24). Yes, doing good should be constantly on our mind and forever in our hearts, and life will be good!

We read the Savior's admonition in Doctrine and Covenants 81:5: "Succor the weak, lift up the hands which hang down, and strengthen the feeble knees." In a crucial battle of the children of Israel against the armies of Amulek, we read of a marvelous application of this principle. "And it came to pass, when Moses held up his hand, that Israel prevailed: and when he let down his hand, Amulek prevailed. But Moses' hands were heavy; and they took a stone, and put it under him, and he sat thereon; and Aaron and Hur stayed up his hands, the one on the one side, and the other on the other side; and his hands were steady until the going down of the sun" (Exodus 17:11–12). President Henry B. Eyring has said, "He [the Lord] has invited and commanded us to participate in His work to lift up those in need. We make a covenant to do that in the waters of baptism and in the holy temples of God. We renew that covenant on Sundays when we partake of the sacrament" ("Opportunities to Do Good," *Ensign* or *Liahona*, May 2011).

The words of a well-known hymn remind us that when we go about doing good, we are on the Lord's errand. "Have I done any good in the world today? / Have I helped anyone in need? . . . / Has anyone's burden been lighter today / Because I was willing to share? . . . / To God each good work will be known. . . . / Doing good is a pleasure, a joy beyond measure, / A blessing of duty and love" ("Have I Done Any Good?" *Hymns*, no 223).

Questions to Ponder

- What is one good thing I will do today, and who will it bless?

Chapter 6

Because of Him We Have a Path to Follow

Our Savior Jesus Christ has given us the way as well as the example to follow. Christ was selfless. He was altruistic. He was noble. He was magnanimous. He was benevolent. He was forgiving. He was a defender of the downtrodden. He was kind and generous. He was a defender of truth. As we read these attributes of Christ, His goodness and grace are personified in His very being. He is the perfect example.

And the Lord has declared, "If any man will come after me, let him deny himself, and *take up his cross, and follow me*" (Matthew 16:24; emphasis added). And He has said, "Therefore I would that ye should be perfect even as I, or your Father who is in heaven is perfect" (3 Nephi 12:48). When we come unto the Lord and follow His path, we can become perfected through Him.

The words of Moroni are empowering and contain many supernal doctrines regarding our being made perfect through Christ.

> Yea, come unto Christ, and be perfected in him, and deny yourselves of all ungodliness; and if ye shall deny yourselves of all ungodliness, and love God with all your might, mind and strength, then is his grace sufficient for you, that by his grace ye may be perfect in Christ; and

if by the grace of God ye are perfect in Christ, ye can in nowise deny the power of God.

And again, if ye by the grace of God are perfect in Christ, and deny not his power, then are ye sanctified in Christ by the grace of God, through the shedding of the blood of Christ, which is in the covenant of the Father unto the remission of your sins, that ye become holy, without spot. (Moroni 10:32–33)

It is through the power of our Savior that we can be made perfect. Nephi explains the process:

Wherefore, my beloved brethren, I know that if ye shall follow the Son, with full purpose of heart, acting no hypocrisy and no deception before God, but with real intent, repenting of your sins, witnessing unto the Father *that ye are willing to take upon you the name of Christ, by baptism*—yea, by following your Lord and your Savior down into the water, according to his word, behold, *then shall ye receive the Holy Ghost*; yea, then cometh the baptism of fire and of the Holy Ghost; and then can ye speak with the tongue of angels, and shout praises unto the Holy One of Israel. (2 Nephi 31:13; emphasis added)

As we faithfully follow this process, we can begin to acquire the attributes of our Beloved Savior Jesus Christ.

Christ Was Selfless

Christ gave His all to His Father's will and His Father's cause, which was His cause as the Anointed Messiah. Never was there a self-centered thought that deterred Him from loving and caring for others. A selfless person is always thinking of others at the expense of their own convenience and comfort. Indeed, when we act in a selfless manner, the many tribulations of life are abated, as Alma explains when he describes the selfless missionary labors of himself and his companion: They took

> no thought for themselves what they should eat, or what they should drink, or what they should put on. And the Lord provided for them that they should hunger not, neither should they thirst; yea, and he also gave them strength, that they should suffer no manner of afflictions, save it were swallowed up in the joy of Christ. Now this was according to the prayer of Alma; and this because he prayed in faith. (Alma 31:37–38)

The Lord served without any thought of reciprocation and always forgave others when they were not at their best—even to the point of taking His life. The willingness to sacrifice is part of the nature of a selfless person. The Lord reminds us,

> But Jesus called them to him, and saith unto them, Ye know that they which are accounted to rule over the Gentiles exercise lordship over them; and their great ones exercise authority upon them. But so shall it not be among you: but whosoever will be great among you, shall be your minister. And whosoever of you will be the chiefest, shall be servant of all. For even the Son of man came not to be ministered unto, but to minister, and to give his life a ransom for many. (Mark 10:42–45)

Becoming selfless requires our hearts to be engaged outside of ourselves and concerned with others' wants and needs. It requires a new thought pattern: "Whom can I serve?" "Whom can I bless?" "Whom can I lift?" "Whom can I comfort?" And then we come to realize that selflessness is part of coming unto Christ through the covenant of baptism and following Him as His disciples as we endure to the end.

And it came to pass that he said unto them: Behold, here are the waters of Mormon (for thus were they called) and now, as ye are desirous to come into the fold of God, and to be called his people, *and are willing to bear one another's burdens*, that they may be light;

Yea, and *are willing to mourn with those that mourn*; yea, *and comfort those that stand in need of comfort, and to stand as witnesses of God at all times and in all things, and in all places that ye may be in, even until death, that ye may* be redeemed of God, and be numbered with those of the first resurrection, that ye may have eternal life. (Mosiah 18:8–9; emphasis added)

As we ponder the previous verses we have heard countless times, we come to realize that we were baptized unto "selflessness." We become selfless in our hearts when we understand and appreciate our covenant with the Lord upon coming into His fold. We give genuine praise and encouragement at every opportunity. Expressions of gratitude become our conversation with others. We look into the eyes of others and let the light of the Lord radiate to them in countless ways. The Lord commanded us to do so. "Therefore let your light so shine before this people, that they may see your good works and glorify your Father who is in heaven" (3 Nephi 12:16). Our good works are empowered by the grace of God that we may bless others and glorify God. We are His glory and His work (see Moses 1:39). In the gospel of John, we learn, "Herein is my Father glorified, that ye bear much fruit; so shall ye be my disciples" (John

Our good works are empowered by the grace of God that we may bless others and glorify God.

15:8).We, like Nephi, should seek the glory of God and the welfare of our brothers and sisters (see 2 Nephi 1:25). Remember, in our desire to become like Christ, we must not forget that we are mortals with frailties and we cannot do all that we might deem necessary. We just do the best we can because the Lord knows our heart, and that is where He looks to know our intent to do good. Selflessness will become our nature as our hearts are filled with charity—a gift from the Father because we are true followers of His Son.

BEWARE OF SELFISHNESS

We must remember that selfishness is the seedbed of countless sins, including the universal sin of pride, envy, jealousy, dishonesty, covetousness, lust, rebellion, hypocrisy, immorality—and the list continues with every conceivable sin.

Of all the destructive forces of pride, nothing is as devastating as selfishness. Selfishness cankers the soul, wreaks havoc in relationships, and makes communication almost nonexistent. In addition, selfishness can lead to feeling lust, being greedy, and seeking for unrighteous power. Of all the negative traits of society and individuals, selfishness is one of the most grievous; therefore, we must all work to overcome it. Selfishness is diametrically opposed to charity, the supreme element in becoming like our Savior Jesus Christ. In the presence of charity, selfishness vanishes. The Apostle Paul explained this most eloquently: "Charity suffereth long, and is kind; charity envieth not; charity vaunteth not itself, is not puffed up" (1 Corinthians 13:4). Let us strive to purge every ounce of selfishness from our hearts until we are filled with the pure love of Christ.

President Hinckley counsels us,

> "Selfishness is the basis of our troubles . . . in this community and in this nation and in the world—a vicious preoccupation with our own comforts, with the satisfaction of our own appetites. . . .

Selfishness is the cause of most of the domestic problems that afflict so many homes of our nation. . . .

So many in the game of life get to first base, or second, or even third, but then fail to score. They are inclined to live unto themselves, denying their generous instincts, grasping for possessions and in their self-centered, uninspired living, sharing neither talent nor faith with others. . . .

The antidote for selfishness is service, a reaching out to those about us—those in the home and those beyond the walls of the home. A child who grows in a home where there is a selfish, grasping father is likely to develop those tendencies in his own life. On the other hand, a child who sees his father and mother forgo comforts for themselves as they reach out to those in distress, will likely follow the same pattern when he or she grows to maturity. (*Teachings of Gordon B. Hinckley* [Salt Lake City: Deseret Book, 1997], 583–584)

Selfishness is the cause of virtually all marital discord. It is evidenced in the inability to communicate and reason together, leading to misunderstandings, unrealized expectations, and demanding behavior, among other things. Selfishness is the destroyer of all relationships.

Now we know why we have covenanted, as disciples of Christ, to follow Him as selfless servants, always thinking of blessing and serving others. This is the essence of living the gospel. We root selfishness out of our very being with charity as it fills our souls with love. Mormon reminds us of the empowering qualities of charity, which never fail.

And charity suffereth long, and is kind, and envieth not, and is not puffed up, seeketh not her own, is not easily provoked, thinketh no evil, and rejoiceth not in iniquity but rejoiceth in the truth, beareth all things, believeth all things, hopeth all things, endureth all things.

Wherefore, my beloved brethren, if ye have not charity, ye are nothing, for charity never faileth. Wherefore, cleave unto charity, which is the greatest of all, for all things must fail—

But charity is the pure love of Christ, and it endureth forever; and whoso is found possessed of it at the last day, it shall be well with him. (Moroni 7:45–47)

Christ Was Magnanimous

Christ was benevolent and willing to give His life that we might live. In His devotion to His Father, He endured the winepress of Gethsemane, the agony of the cross of Golgotha, and arose triumphant from the Garden Tomb. He fulfilled His messianic calling and redeemed us from our lost and fallen state. He made possible our perfection if we would come unto Him with full purpose of heart, offering our sacrifice of a broken heart and contrite spirit.

There was complete submission in the hours of agony in Gethsemane, for He was doing what He was foreordained to do: the will of the Father in our behalf. "For behold, blood cometh from every pore, so great shall be his anguish for the wickedness and the abominations of his people" (Mosiah 3:7). The Lord explains His purpose and the price of redemption:

Behold I have given unto you my gospel, and this is the gospel which I have given unto you—that I came into the world to do the will of my Father, because my Father sent me.

And my Father sent me that I might be lifted up upon the cross; and after that I had been lifted up upon the

> cross, that I might draw all men unto me, that as I have been lifted up by men even so should men be lifted up by the Father, to stand before me, to be judged of their works, whether they be good or whether they be evil—
>
> And for this cause have I been lifted up; therefore, according to the power of the Father I will draw all men unto me, that they may be judged according to their works. (3 Nephi 27:13–15)

From the cross He uttered, "Father, forgive them; for they know not what they do" (Luke 23:34). He was ever an example of godliness and goodness while in the depths of suffering in agony to pay the debt of our sins. To comprehend this supreme act of goodness, we should consider the pain and agony in Gethsemane and what He endured as He was crucified on the cross.

The crucifixion form of execution was purported to have been invented by the Persians in approximately 300 B.C.; however, there are records indicating the use of crucifixion for executions as early as the sixth century B.C., and the Romans finalized the process. Constantine, the Roman Emperor, later abolished crucifixion as a form of execution in the Roman Empire in A.D. 337 out of respect for the Savior.

The pain inflicted upon the victim was excruciating, and that is where the word *excruciating* originated (Latin, *excruciatus*, or "out of the cross"). It was a slow and agonizingly painful death. The body was nailed to the cross, and in the case of the Savior, there were nails in the palms of His hands, in His wrists, and in His feet. These nails, according to archeological data, were tapered iron spikes between five to seven inches in length. The nails through the Savior's wrists were near to or pierced the median nerve, which would be stimulated with any movement, and then horrific shocks would send tremors throughout His body. The nails in the Lord's feet would have been placed through both feet as they were placed on top of one another and pierced through the metatarsal space.

Christ was benevolent and willing to give His life that we might live.

As Christ hung on the cross, He was surely bleeding from His scourging, and the loss of blood only exacerbated His pain and weakness. When He could no longer bear His weight by pushing up from His feet, surely His shoulder joints became separated due to the weight of his body. On the cross, the Savior's breathing was severely hampered and the muscle cramping continuously prevented the full respiration cycle. The mere act of breathing evoked pain either in His chest or in His body as He attempted to raise up high enough to get a full breath of air. The feeling of suffocation and the inability to get enough air often led to asphyxia, which was one of the many factors leading to death by crucifixion. Dehydration and cardiovascular problems (especially heart arrhythmia and congestive heart failure and plural effusions or discharges) all contributed to death. It was a slow form of dying, often lasting several hours, or even days, all of which is not only agonizing and excruciating but was also physiologically impossible to bear. With all the precursors of death weighing upon the Lord's body, it seems that eventually His heart gave out. Describing the Lord's death on the cross, James E. Talmage says, "The present writer believes that the Lord Jesus died of a broken heart. The psalmist sang in dolorous measure according to his inspired prevision of the Lord's passion: 'Reproach hath broken my heart; and I am full of heaviness: and I looked for some to take pity, but there was none; and for comforters, but I found none . . .' (Psalms 69:20, 21; see also 22:14)" (*Jesus the Christ* [Salt Lake City: The Church of Jesus Christ of Latter-day Saints, 1981], 669). And standing at the base of the cross, witnessing the death of her beloved Son, stood Mary with her sister, Mary (the wife of Cleophas), and Mary Magdalene, along with John the Beloved. The spear pierced His side and blood and water came forth. Our Beloved Savior had finished His work on Golgotha's hill.

Don and Jay Parry in their epic work on the Atonement of Christ have written,

> Why did the Romans use a cross for their executions? It is likely that it was the most horrible form of suffering they were able to devise. . . . If the Romans used crucifixion because it was so dreadful a way to die, why did the Father require the Son to die in such a manner? The following are some possibilities:
>
> First, it was required that the Son descend below all things. The descent brought together a combination of the intense suffering in the Garden of Gethsemane, the sleepless night, the deep pain of betrayal, the sadistic treatment of the Romans and Jews, the brutality of the cross, the spiritual death of a sinless being, and more— all combined in an emotionally heightened state that has sometimes, with meaning, been called "the passion."
>
> Second, death by crucifixion represented a curse on the victim. Paul wrote, "Christ hath redeemed us from the curse of the law, being made a curse for us: for it is written, Cursed is every one that hangeth on a tree" (Gal. 3:13). Thus, in submitting himself to crucifixion, Jesus Christ was "made a curse for us," in keeping with the pronouncement in the law of Moses: "And if a man have committed a sin worthy of death, and he be to be put to death, and thou hang him on a tree: His body shall not remain all night upon the tree, but thou shalt in any wise bury him that day; (for he that is hanged is accursed of God . . .)" (Deut. 21:22–23).
>
> Third, the symbolism of crucifixion is instructive. The arms are reached out as in surrender. The crucified individual

was forced into that position and held there by the cruelest of means—but Christ willingly drank of this portion of the bitter cup, that the will of the Father might be done in every detail. (Donald W. Parry, Jay A. Parry, *Symbols and Shadows: Unlocking a Deeper Understanding of the Atonement* [Salt Lake City, Desert Book, 2009], 234–35)

Understanding and appreciating what literally happened in death by crucifixion can increase our empathy for our Beloved Savior. As we conclude this section, remember that every moment of His Atoning sacrifice brought agony to our Beloved Savior. My heart is heavy and my mind is overloaded as I try to comprehend and feel enough gratitude for all that my Savior went through for me and for you.

Our minds are not able to comprehend all things, but we can still be grateful and recognize our total dependence on our Savior Jesus Christ. We need to grow through faith, hope, and charity, with an eye single to the glory of God. We need to love our Father and our Savior with all our heart, might, mind, and strength. If we ponder just a little, we will readily see what Moses came to understand. "For this cause I know that man is nothing, which thing I never had supposed" (Moses 1:10). This is what Paul was trying to teach the Galatians: "For if a man think himself to be something, when he is nothing, he deceiveth himself" (Galatians 6:3). Moses and Paul were not teaching that we as the divine children of God are nothing; quite the contrary. They were teaching that we, in our fallen state, are spiritually lost and fallen and completely dependent upon the grace of God. This is why Ammon said, "Yea, I know that I am nothing; as to my strength I am weak; therefore I will not boast of myself, but I will boast of my God, for in his strength I can do all things" (Alma 26:12). In this state of mortality, we have to live by faith. Our power comes as we exercise faith in the Lord Jesus Christ and His atoning sacrifice, "[humbling ourselves] even in the depths of humility, calling on the name of the Lord daily, and standing steadfastly in the faith" (Mosiah 4:11). Priesthood power operates by faith and in the name of Jesus Christ, through which all things can be done.

Our dependence on God our Father and our Savior Jesus Christ was and is part of the Plan. Our dependence upon God the Father and our Savior Jesus Christ draws us to Them as we recognize our own nothingness and unworthiness (see Mosiah 4:5; Alma 38:14; Helaman 12:7).

We are ever grateful for the grace of God the Father and our Savior Jesus Christ. As our empathy increases, so will our gratitude and our love for our Heavenly Father and our Savior.

Through empathy we can begin to get a glimpse into the greatness of the soul of Christ and embrace this overriding truth . . . everything is *because of Him.* Oh, what gratitude and love should come from the depths of our souls for the goodness of the Lord. This should inspire us to follow Him with increased dedication.

CHRIST WAS KIND AND GENEROUS

If anyone was downtrodden, the Savior was their protector and advocate. He never allowed petty resentfulness or vindictiveness to be part of His response. And in His magnanimity, He was ever forgiving and protective of the less fortunate. He was loving and kind and generous in every facet of His life. What does it take to always be kind and generous? What is the element of character that enables us to always show loving-kindness and generosity to others? It is charity—the pure love of Christ.

The Lord is ever willing to help us acquire this heavenly virtue. As we reread the following verse, remember that repetition is the Lord's way of teaching and learning. Mormon describes thirteen elements of charity. "And charity *suffereth long,* and *is kind,* and *envieth not,* and *is not puffed up, seeketh not her own, is not easily provoked, thinketh no evil,* and *rejoiceth not in iniquity* but *rejoiceth in the truth, beareth all things, believeth all things, hopeth all things, endureth all things*" (Moroni 7:45; emphasis added).

Our power comes as we exercise faith in the Lord Jesus Christ and His atoning sacrifice.

Let these words penetrate our heart and mind so they become embedded in our very soul: "And beside this, giving all diligence, add to your faith virtue; and to virtue knowledge; and to knowledge temperance; and to temperance patience; and to patience godliness; and to godliness brotherly kindness; and to brotherly kindness charity" (2 Peter 1:5–7).

In this scripture, Peter describes a step-by-step process toward receiving the divine nature of Christ and being filled with charity. Being kind and generous requires that we seek after the gift of charity. God the Father will bestow this precious gift upon us as we pray with all the energy of heart and become true followers of His Beloved Son (see Moroni 7:48).

The pure love of Christ would suggest that we become charitable in our daily life. The following verses need no commentary—just a place in our hearts.

- "Freely ye have received, freely give." (Matthew 10:8)

- "He answereth and saith unto them, He that hath two coats, let him impart to him that hath none; and he that hath meat, let him do likewise." (Luke 3:11)

- "But when thou makest a feast, call the poor, the maimed, the lame, the blind: and thou shalt be blessed; for they cannot recompense thee: for thou shalt be recompensed at the resurrection of the just." (Luke 14:13–14)

- "Think of your brethren like unto yourselves, and be familiar with all and free with your substance, that they may be rich like unto you." (Jacob 2:17)

- "And again Alma commanded that the people of the church should impart of their substance, every one according to that which he had; if he have more abundantly he should impart more abundantly; and of him that had but little, but little should be required; and to him that had not should be given.

    "And thus they should impart of their substance of their own free will and good desires towards God, and to those priests that stood in need, yea, and to every needy, naked soul." (Mosiah 18:27–28)

- "Therefore, if ye do not remember to be charitable, ye are as dross, which the refiners do cast out, (it being of no worth) and is trodden under foot of men." (Alma 34:29)

As I reread those verses for the umpteenth time, I vowed to be more generous. Remember, never deny a generous thought, for it will always lead to loving-kindness. Yes, we are commanded to be loving and kind and generous toward all mankind. Why? Because love of God and our fellow men are the two great commandments (see Matthew 22:36–40). And the commandments all come with promised blessings. When we have charity, we are the worthy sons and daughters of God and can come into His presence. Mormon lovingly entreats us, "That when he shall appear we shall be like him, for we shall see him as he is; that we may have this hope; that we may be purified even as he is pure. Amen" (Moroni 7:48).

Christ Was a Defender of Truth

The Lord fearlessly defended the truth; gospel truths outranked customs of the day. He dined with sinners, healed on the Sabbath, and rebuked the Jewish hierarchy for their hypocrisy (see Matthew: 1–16; Mark 2:23–28). Forgiveness and mercy are our mandates; judgment is for the Lord, as He so beautifully demonstrated with the woman taken in adultery (see John 8:7). Knowing the sanctity of the Lord's holy house, He would not let the ruling class make it a den of thieves (see Matthew 21:12–13). Hypocrisy was high on the list of grievous sins which the Lord condemned (see Matthew 23:13–29; Luke 12:1). His example bids us to stand for truth and righteousness. "Be strong and of a good courage" (Joshua 1:6). We should be like Moroni, the chief captain of the Nephite armies, who was a man of courage. He fought for righteousness (see Alma 46:12–13).

There is a price to be paid in standing for truth and righteousness, and it outweighs all the criticism and vicissitudes that can be thrust upon us.

Our Savior freely and serenely accepted His role of Savior and Redeemer. He was spit upon, scourged, mocked, and belittled, yet He knew His destiny. He suffered for the will of the Father. Nothing was too hard for the Lord, for He knew who He was and His anointed role as the promised Messiah: "I am the way, the truth, and the life: no man cometh unto the Father, but by me" (John 14:6). The Lord reminds us, "Greater love hath no man than this, that a man lay down his life for his friends" (John 15:13).

Defending the freedom of others is a selfless thing to do. This is what made Captain Moroni so good. We may not be required to lay down our lives but rather to live a life of service. Assist the lonely and struggling. Lift those who are downtrodden. Mourn with those who mourn. Our office and calling as Saints requires us to "be faithful; stand in the office which I have appointed unto you; succor the weak, lift up the hands which hang down, and strengthen the feeble knees" (Doctrine and Covenants 81:5). The Lord reminds us that we are to "strengthen [our] brethren in all [our] conversation, in all [our] prayers, in all [our] exhortations, and in all [our] doings" (Doctrine and Covenants 108:7). We become defenders of the truth because we stand for truth and righteousness. Because of Him, we seek to do as Jesus would do, for this is the price of discipleship.

Questions to Ponder

- How does knowledge and understanding of Christ's attributes help me move along the Lord's pathway in life?

- What can I do today to embrace the attributes of Christ?

Chapter 7

BECAUSE OF HIM WE HAVE GOSPEL VALUES

WHEN WE UNDERSTAND AND APPRECIATE what matters most, the values within the gospel of Jesus Christ come to the forefront of our lives. President Hinckley has said, "I see a wonderful future in a very uncertain world. *If we will cling to our values,* if we will build on our inheritance, if we will walk in obedience before the Lord, if we will simply live the gospel we will be blessed in a magnificent and wonderful way. We will be looked upon as a peculiar people who have found the key to a peculiar happiness" ("Look to the Future," *Ensign,* Nov. 1997; emphasis added).

When values are firmly in place, our lives have direction because we choose to follow Christ. The Lord has said, "No man can serve two masters: for either he will hate the one, and love the other; or else he will hold to the one, and despise the other. Ye cannot serve God and mammon" (Matthew 6:24). So how do we serve God? The Lord went on to say, "But seek ye first the kingdom of God, and his righteousness; and all these things shall be added unto you" (Matthew 6:33). Quite simply put, we are to seek to build up the kingdom of God! The kingdom of God is composed of people. Therefore, we should seek to bless others and bring souls unto Christ. We have to choose because we cannot live a duplicitous life. Because of the mercurial nature of man, we struggle as we seek worldly pleasures at the expense of things that matter most. The Lord has set a standard of values that can lead to happiness, and there is no other way.

The scriptures are replete with examples of people choosing the wrong path. We read of the parable of the good Samaritan, where a Levite and a priest passed up the opportunity to rescue a man who fell among thieves (see Luke 10:30–32). In another instance, the Lord invited several people to His special marriage feast, but many of them had other plans and made excuses for not coming. They had other things to do. The old triad of choices was in front of them—good, better, and best. If our values and priorities are misplaced, we will miss what matters most in our lives—doing the will of God.

> *The Lord has set a standard of values that can lead to happiness, and there is no other way.*

The price of discipleship is high and requires us to make righteous choices. The parable of the sower is a great example of the status of the hearts of men when the word of God is sowed among them. "He also that received seed among the thorns is he that heareth the word; and the care of this world, and the deceitfulness of riches, choke the word, and he becometh unfruitful" (Matthew 13:22). Indeed, it was the cares of the world and riches that caused the word NOT to take root in his heart.

The commandments, covenants, standards, and values of the gospel of Jesus Christ must be written in our hearts. "Forasmuch as ye are manifestly declared to be the epistle of Christ ministered by us, written not with ink, but with the Spirit of the living God; not in tables of stone, but in fleshy tables of the heart" (2 Corinthians 3:3).

Isaiah records, "Hearken unto me, ye that know righteousness, the people in whose heart I have written my law, fear ye not the reproach of men, neither be ye afraid of their revilings" (2 Nephi 8:7).

The Lord's Sermon on the Mount makes things perfectly clear: "Lay not up for yourselves treasures upon earth, where moth and rust doth corrupt, and where thieves break through and steal: But lay up for your-selves treasures in heaven, where neither moth nor rust doth corrupt, and where thieves do not break through nor steal: for where your treasure is, there will your heart be also" (Matthew 6:19–21).

Nephi, the son of Helaman, taught this doctrine and the consequences of disobedience: "But behold, ye have rejected the truth, and rebelled against your holy God; and even at this time, instead of laying up for yourselves treasures in heaven, where nothing doth corrupt, and where nothing can come which is unclean, ye are heaping up for yourselves wrath against the day of judgment" (Helaman 8:25).

The Lord reminds us,

> If any man will come after me, let him deny himself, and take up his cross, and follow me. For whosoever will save his life shall lose it: and whosoever will lose his life for my sake shall find it. For what is a man profited, if he shall gain the whole world, and lose his own soul? or what shall a man give in exchange for his soul? For the Son of man shall come in the glory of his Father with his angels; and then he shall reward every man according to his works. (Matthew 16:24–27)

If we have eyes to see and hearts to feel and minds to comprehend, we will see the merit of the gospel plan in every aspect of our lives. We must not compartmentalize the gospel in our lives; rather, we must live the gospel in every facet of our lives. The benefit of living the gospel and internalizing its values is life eternal. There is no other way save it be through the kingdom of God and all the ordinances and covenants contained therein and administered by His holy priesthood. The kingdom of God on earth is The Church of Jesus Christ of Latter-day Saints.

The Lord sacrificed all for the children of God the Father in every land. His life was swallowed up in the will of the Father. He knew the value and worth of the souls of mankind . . . they were "great in the sight of God" (Doctrine and Covenants 18:10). The Lord was sent to heal the brokenhearted (see Luke 4:18). He speaks of those being converted, and then He will heal them and make them whole: "And after their temptations, and much tribulation, behold, I, the Lord, will feel after them, and if they harden not their hearts, and stiffen not their necks against me, *they shall be converted, and I will heal them*" (Doctrine and Covenants 112:13; emphasis added). To be converted and healed is to be changed and purified through the Lord's infinite Atonement so our beliefs, our heart, and our life are in harmony with the will of God and we are freed from the burden of sin. Indeed, we are made whole through the merits of Christ the Lord.

The Lord reminds us in our quest to rescue the lost and struggling souls, "Nevertheless, ye shall not cast him out of your synagogues, or your places of worship, for unto such shall ye continue to minister; for ye know not but what they will return and repent, and come unto me with full purpose of heart, *and I shall heal them*; and ye shall be the means of bringing salvation unto them" (3 Nephi 18:32; emphasis added). We can be saviors on mount Zion, instruments in the hands of the Lord, to assist in bringing souls unto Him. As we follow Christ, we are truly *"fishers of men"* (Matthew 4:19; emphasis added). Remember, the last words of Christ to Peter, the chief Apostle, were, "Feed my sheep" (John 21:17). Souls are precious. The Lord's values should be our values, and thus, His will becomes our will. As we become unified, we will become one with the Father and the Son (see John 17).

Becoming One with the Father and the Son

The Lord in His great intercessory prayer petitioned the Father in our behalf.

> And now I am no more in the world, but these are in the world, and I come to thee. Holy Father, keep through thine own name those whom thou hast given me, that they may be one, as we are . . . .
>
> Neither pray I for these alone, but for them also which shall believe on me through their word;

That they all may be one; as thou, Father, art in me, and I in thee, that they also may be one in us: that the world may believe that thou hast sent me.

And the glory which thou gavest me I have given them; that they may be one, even as we are one:

I in them, and thou in me, that they may be made perfect in one; and that the world may know that thou hast sent me, and hast loved them, as thou hast loved me. . . .

And I have declared unto them thy name, and will declare it: that the love wherewith thou hast loved me may be in them, and I in them. (John 17:11, 20–23, 26)

This oneness is what the Lord prays for and expects from us. "I say unto you, be one; and if ye are not one ye are not mine" (Doctrine and Covenants 38:27). We should pray that our mind and heart, even our very will, will become the will of God the Father and our Savior Jesus Christ. As we become totally aligned with the Father and the Son, we joyfully submit our will and our life to please God. We become empowered by the grace of God.

When our hearts are knit together in becoming one with the Father and the Son, our lives become centered on the Father and the Son . . . to do Their will and to bring souls unto Christ and ultimately to the Father. Our will is swallowed up in the joy of the Lord.

This oneness and unity is vital to our families. When we have unity, there will be no contention. Agreed-upon values will always lead to the oneness and unity of the family.

When we have unity,
there will be no contention.

Questions to Ponder

- What are two ways that I can write good values on my heart?

- What is one treasure I have as a result of the values I hold?

Chapter 8

BECAUSE OF HIM WE CAN HAVE HAPPINESS AND JOY

HEAVENLY FATHER AND THE SAVIOR seek for us to be happy and find joy in our lives. The love of God, which is the fruit of the tree of life, is desirable above all other things to make one happy. The Prophet Joseph has stated, "Happiness is the object and design of our existence; and will be the end thereof, if we pursue the path that leads to it; *and this path is virtue, uprightness, faithfulness, holiness, and keeping all the commandments of God*" (quoted in James E. Faust, "Our Search for Happiness," *Ensign*, Oct. 2000; emphasis added).

Joy is a blessing from the Lord. We shouted for *joy* as we accepted the plan of redemption (see Job 38:7). The angel of the Lord declared, "Fear not: for, behold, *I bring you good tidings of great joy*, which shall be to all people" (Luke 2:10; emphasis added). Through our faithful efforts, the Lord rewards us with joy: "Thou hast been faithful over a few things, I will make thee ruler over many things: enter thou into the *joy of thy lord*" (Matthew 25:21; emphasis added). We are blessed by our persecutions. "Rejoice ye in that day, and leap for joy: for, behold, your reward is great in heaven: for in the like manner did their fathers unto the prophets" (Luke 6:23).

John the Baptist found joy in being the forerunner of Christ (see John 3:28–29). His joy was in his Lord. The meek and lowly find joy in the heavenly virtues and things of an eternal nature. The Lord, in a most caring, loving, and perfect way, taught how He felt about us and our well-being when He said, "If ye keep my commandments, ye shall abide in my love; even as I have kept my Father's commandments, and abide in his love. These things have I spoken unto you, that my joy might remain in you, and that your joy might be full" (John 15:10–11). Our joy comes through Christ and His infinite Atonement, for our sorrows are swallowed up in Him. "But rejoice, inasmuch as ye are partakers of Christ's sufferings; that, when his glory shall be revealed, ye may be glad also with exceeding joy" (1 Peter 4:13).

We begin to see that our joy is connected to the grace of God and His gifts through His Beloved Son and through the Holy Ghost. "The kingdom of God is . . . righteousness, and peace, and joy in the Holy Ghost" (Romans 14:17). And the Apostle Paul again reminds us that "the fruit of the Spirit is *love, joy, peace, longsuffering, gentleness, goodness, faith*" (Galatians 5:22; emphasis added), an impressive and humbling affirmation of our Savior's love and the blessings that come from Him through the power of the Holy Ghost. The Holy Ghost is indeed the unspeakable gift that empowers us to do all things. "God shall give unto you knowledge by his Holy Spirit, yea, by the unspeakable gift of the Holy Ghost, that has not been revealed since the world was until now" (Doctrine and Covenants 121:26). And through the power of the Holy Ghost, we are blessed in every aspect of our lives.

Now we can understand and appreciate the following statement by President Wilford Woodruff: "You may have the administration of angels, you may see many miracles; you may see many wonders in the earth; but I claim that the gift of the Holy Ghost is the greatest gift that can be bestowed upon man" (*The Discourses of Wilford Woodruff*, sel. G. Homer Durham [Salt Lake City: Bookcraft, 1946], 5). And it came from the Father because we believe in His Beloved Son, who makes all things possible. "Father, thou hast given them the Holy Ghost because they believe in me" (3 Nephi 19:22).

President Brigham Young also emphasized the blessings of the fulness of the Holy Ghost when he said, "If the Latter-day Saints will walk up to their privileges, and exercise faith in the name of Jesus Christ, and live in the enjoyment of the fullness of the Holy Ghost constantly day by day, there is nothing on the face of the earth that they could ask for, that would not be given to them. The Lord is waiting to be very gracious unto this people, and to pour out upon them riches, honor, glory, and power, even that they may possess all things according to the promises He has made through His apostles and prophets" (*Journal of Discourses*, 26 vols., 1867, 11:114).

How I treasure the gift of the Holy Ghost in my life. I feel it and am literally transformed by a desire to do good, because doing so leads me to do more good. When I think of others, I seem to have a greater abundance of the Spirit, thus a greater abundance of joy. It was this power that God the Father gave to His Son. "God anointed Jesus of Nazareth with the Holy Ghost and with power: who went about doing good, and healing all that were oppressed of the devil; for God was with him" (Acts 10:38).

Let us remember that the Holy Ghost will bestow upon us the feelings of joy. "I will impart unto you of my Spirit, which shall enlighten your mind, which shall fill your soul with joy" (Doctrine and Covenants 11:13). With this scripture embedded in our mind and heart, we see the relationship between life, the Holy Ghost, and joy, as Lehi taught, "Adam fell that men might be; and men are, that they might have joy" (2 Nephi 2:25). We are meant to have joy in this life. We are meant to know joy, which comes from loving the Lord and keeping His commandments. As we trust the Savior and lay hold on His Atonement, we can partake of this joy.

King Benjamin explained the repentance process, which brings about this exceeding great joy. "And it came to pass that after they had spoken these words the Spirit of the Lord came upon them, and they were filled with joy, having received a remission of their sins, and having peace of conscience, because of the exceeding faith which they had in Jesus Christ who should come, according to the words which king Benjamin had spoken unto them" (Mosiah 4:3). In the remission of our sins, we pray with godly sorrow and the Lord rewards us: "If thou art sorrowful, call on the Lord thy God with supplication, that your souls may be joyful" (Doctrine and Covenants 136:29; see also 2 Samuel 22:7).

Following the sermon of King Benjamin, many souls began to repent, and they began praying: "And behold, even at this time, ye have been calling on his name, and begging for a remission of your sins. And has he suffered that ye have begged in vain? Nay; he has poured out his Spirit upon you, and has caused that your hearts should be filled with joy, and has caused that your mouths should be stopped that ye could not find utterance, so exceedingly great was your joy" (Mosiah 4:20). Yes, a fullness of joy comes to us as we come unto Christ and receive the blessings of grace from the Father and the Son.

A fullness of joy comes to us as we come unto Christ and receive the blessings of grace.

The Lord feels joy as He observes our spiritual growth, as was noted in His visit to the Nephites: "And they arose from the earth, and he said unto them: Blessed are ye because of your faith. And now behold, my joy is full" (3 Nephi 17:20). "And none of them are lost; and in them I have fulness of joy" (3 Nephi 27:31). We begin to see that the fruit of righteousness is happiness and joy. Alma attempted to explain his joy when he was in the midst of repenting:

> And now, behold, when I thought this, I could remember my pains no more; yea, I was harrowed up by the memory of my sins no more. And oh, what joy, and what marvelous light I did behold; yea, my soul was filled with joy as exceeding as was my pain! Yea, I say unto you, my

son, that there could be nothing so exquisite and so bitter as were my pains. Yea, and again I say unto you, my son, that on the other hand, there can be nothing so exquisite and sweet as was my joy. (Alma 36:19–21)

Seeing the joy the Lord feels when a sinner repents teaches us a transcending truth about the worth of souls in the eyes of the Lord.

Remember the worth of souls is great in the sight of God;

For, behold, the Lord your Redeemer suffered death in the flesh; wherefore he suffered the pain of all men, that all men might repent and come unto him.

And he hath risen again from the dead, that he might bring all men unto him, on conditions of repentance.

And how great is his joy in the soul that repenteth!

Wherefore, you are called to cry repentance unto this people.

And if it so be that you should labor all your days in crying repentance unto this people, and bring, *save it be one soul unto me, how great shall be your joy with him in the kingdom of my Father!*

And now, *if your joy will be great with one soul that you have brought unto me into the kingdom of my Father, how great will be your joy if you should bring many souls unto me!* (Doctrine and Covenants 18:10–16; emphasis added)

Joy is an attribute of the Master's being and the nature of His godliness. He wants us to have a life of joy. The Lord reminds us, "And whoso is found a faithful, a just, and a wise steward shall enter into the joy of his Lord, and shall inherit eternal life" (Doctrine and Covenants 51:19). In the resurrection of the just, we receive a fulness of joy (see Doctrine and Covenants 93:33), for our fulness of joy is in the Lord (see Doctrine and Covenants 101:36). "And the Lord showed Enoch all things, even unto the end of the world; and he saw the day of the righteous, the hour of their redemption, and received a fulness of joy" (Moses 7:67).

Christ the Lord is joyful because His life is always focused on others.

Christ the Lord is joyful because His life is always focused on others. Every deed He does, every sermon He preaches, and every thought He thinks is motivated by His desire to bless Heavenly Father's children. And when we seek to have this joy within our souls, we will do likewise, as exemplified by Alma and the sons of Mosiah:

> And it came to pass that as Ammon was going forth into the land, that he and his brethren met Alma, over in the place of which has been spoken; and behold, this was a *joyful* meeting.
>
> Now the joy of Ammon was so great even that he was full; yea, he was swallowed up in *the joy of his God*, even to the exhausting of his strength; and he fell again to the earth.
>
> Now was not this *exceeding joy*? Behold, this is joy which none receiveth save it be the truly penitent and humble seeker of happiness.
>
> Now *the joy of Alma* in meeting his brethren was truly great, and also *the joy of Aaron, of Omner, and Himni*; but behold their joy was not that to exceed their strength. (Alma 27:16–19; emphasis added)

Mormon's commendation to the sons of Mosiah and their companions echoes the joy for their Christlike service when he said, "And this is the account of Ammon and his brethren, their journeyings in the land of Nephi, their sufferings in the land, their sorrows, and their afflictions, *and their incomprehensible joy,* and the reception and safety of the brethren in the land of Jershon. And now may the Lord, the Redeemer of all men, bless their souls forever" (Alma 28:8; emphasis added).

Let our lives be driven by these thoughts of Alma, and we too will find joy.

> I know that which the Lord hath commanded me, and I glory in it. I do not glory of myself, but I glory in that which the Lord hath commanded me; yea, and this is my glory, that perhaps I may be an instrument in the hands of God to bring some soul to repentance; *and this is my joy.*
>
> And behold, *when I see many of my brethren truly penitent, and coming to the Lord their God, then is my soul filled with joy;* then do I remember what the Lord has done for me, yea, even that he hath heard my prayer; yea, then do I remember his merciful arm which he extended towards me. (Alma 29:9–10; emphasis added)

And because of Him we shall have joy and we will remember the goodness and mercy of the Lord, and all our trials and tribulations will be "swallowed up in the joy of [our] God" (Alma 27:17).

Questions to Ponder

- What things do I need to do so I have an abundance of joy in my life?

Chapter 9

Because of Him We Can Receive All That the Father Has

And Then They Shall Be Gods

When we receive the Lord, His priesthood, and His word through His servants, we can receive all that the Father has. "And also all they who receive this priesthood receive me, saith the Lord; for he that receiveth my servants receiveth me; and he that receiveth me receiveth my Father; and he that receiveth my Father receiveth my Father's kingdom; therefore all that my Father hath shall be given unto him" (Doctrine and Covenants 84:35–38). And the Lord has said, "And they shall pass by the angels, and the gods, which are set there, to their exaltation and glory in all things, as hath been sealed upon their heads, which glory shall be a fulness and a continuation of the seeds forever and ever. Then shall they be gods, because they have no end" (Doctrine and Covenants 132:19–20). This is what Heavenly Father and our Savior Jesus Christ envision for us.

The Scriptures Teach That We Can Become Gods

"The Spirit itself beareth witness with our spirit, that we are the children of God: and if children, then heirs; heirs of God, and joint-heirs with Christ; if so be that we suffer with him, that we may be also glorified together" (Romans 8:16–17; see also Galatians 4:7; Doctrine and Covenants 88:107).

"For in him we live, and move, and have our being; as certain also of your own poets have said, For we are also his offspring" (Acts 17:28). As children of God, we are heirs of God and joint-heirs with Christ to receive the glory of God. "Therefore I would that ye should be perfect even as I, or your Father who is in heaven is perfect" (3 Nephi 12:48). With these words, the Lord makes it clear that the hope of the Father and the Son is that we may become perfect and complete even as He and our Father are perfect. Our perfection is made possible through the great plan of our Father, through Christ the Lord (see Moroni 10:32–33).

The Lord taught this truth during His mortal ministry, much to the consternation of the Jews. "The Jews answered him, saying, For a good work we stone thee not; but for blasphemy; and because that thou, being a man, makest thyself God. Jesus answered them, Is it not written in your law, I said, Ye are gods" (John 10:33–34)?

The Savior was probably referring to the Old Testament, where the Psalmist said, "I have said, Ye are gods; and all of you are children of the most High" (Psalms 82:6). In the revelation to the Prophet Joseph concerning the celestial degree of glory we learn, "Wherefore, as it is written, they are gods, even the sons of God—wherefore, all things are theirs, whether life or death, or things present, or things to come, all are theirs and they are Christ's, and Christ is God's" (Doctrine and Covenants 76:58–59). We can become like the Father and the Son. The scriptures clearly teach this doctrine. We read in 1 John 3:2, "Beloved, now are we the sons of God, and it doth not yet appear what we shall be: but we know that, when he shall appear, we shall be like him; for we shall see him as he is." And Mormon tells us, "Wherefore, my beloved brethren, pray unto the Father with all the energy of heart, that ye may be filled with this love, which he hath bestowed upon all who are true followers of his Son, Jesus Christ; that ye may become the sons of God; that when he shall appear we shall be like him, for we shall see him as he is; that we may have this hope; that we may be purified even as he is pure. Amen" (Moroni 7:48).

John and Mormon have made it perfectly clear that when we become the sons and daughters of God (see 3 Nephi 9:17) through our faithfulness, and then when we see the Lord, we will be like Him. This is our hope—to become like unto the Lord. This was the promise made to the Three Nephites. "And for this cause (bringing souls to Christ) ye shall have fulness of joy; and ye shall sit down in the kingdom of my Father; yea, your joy shall be full, even as the Father hath given me fulness of joy; and ye shall be even as I am, and I am even as the Father; and the Father and I are one" (3 Nephi 28:10; parentheses added).

The Savior tells us, "For if you keep my commandments you shall receive of his fulness, and be glorified in me as I am in the Father; therefore, I say unto you, you shall receive grace for grace" (Doctrine and Covenants 93:20). And again, we read His holy promise: "Then shall they be gods, because they have no end; therefore shall they be from everlasting to everlasting, because they continue; then shall they be above all, because all things are subject unto them. Then shall they be gods, because they have all power, and the angels are subject unto them" (Doctrine and Covenants 132:20).

It is clear from the foregoing revelations given to the Prophet Joseph that when we are faithful in keeping the commandments, we receive the fullness of our Father and all that He has will be given unto us. With our finite mortal minds, we can read these words, but when struck with the reality—that we can receive all and become like our Father—it is difficult to grasp the infinite power and glory that can be ours. The timeline of becoming perfect even as He is is a lifelong and even an eternal process leading to an inevitable event in our Father's perfect and loving plan. The Lord has decreed, "According to that which was ordained in the midst of the Council of the Eternal God of all other gods before this world was,

It is difficult to grasp the infinite power and glory that can be ours.

that should be reserved unto the finishing and the end thereof, when every man shall enter into his eternal presence and into his immortal rest. How long can rolling waters remain impure? What power shall stay the heavens? As well might man stretch forth his puny arm to stop the Missouri river in its decreed course, or to turn it up stream, as to hinder the Almighty from pouring down knowledge from heaven upon the heads of the Latter-day Saints" (Doctrine and Covenants 121:32–33).

Sister Jennifer C. Lane in her article in *Religious Educator* has given insightful information about "sitting enthroned." It is about becoming what we, as children of God, have the capacity to become. The scriptures tell us to "shake thyself from the dust; arise, sit down" (2 Nephi 8:25). This "sit down" has reference to sitting in the presence of God and "is tied to the images of being with and like God" (Jennifer Lane, "Sitting Enthroned: A Scriptural Perspective," *Religious Educator*, vol. 19, no. 1, 2018; 103–117). Alma's words to the people of Gideon are precious when he said, "And may the Lord bless you, and keep your garments spotless, that ye may at last be brought to *sit down with Abraham, Isaac, and Jacob,* and the holy prophets who have been ever since the world began, having your garments spotless even as their garments are spotless, in the kingdom of heaven to go no more out" (Alma 7:25; emphasis added). Those two words *sit down* have far-reaching connotations. When we sit down with Abraham, Isaac, and Jacob, we must remember, "And because [Abraham, Isaac, and Jacob] did none other things than that which they were commanded, they have entered into their exaltation, according to the promises, and sit upon thrones, and are not angels but are gods" (Doctrine and Covenants 132:37). Alma spoke of this same blessing in his words to Shiblon: "And may the Lord bless your soul, and receive you at the last day into his kingdom, to sit down in peace. Now go, my son, and teach the word unto this people. Be sober. My son, farewell" (Alma 38:15). Amulek, as well as Alma, speaks of this doctrine (see Alma 34:35–36).

Now when you see the words *sit down* in the scriptures, a new vision of becoming like God will be yours (see Lane, "Sitting Enthroned").

The Prophets Have Echoed These Supernal Truths about Becoming Gods

The Prophet Joseph taught prior to his martyrdom the following: "You have got to learn how to be Gods yourselves; and to be kings and priests to God, the same as all Gods have done; by going from a small degree to another, from grace to grace, from exaltation to exaltation" (Joseph Smith, Jr. in "Conference Minutes," *Times and Seasons* [Nauvoo: John Taylor, August 15, 1844; minutes from a talk delivered on April, 1844], 5:614).

The Prophet Joseph also taught,

> God himself was once as we are now, and is an exalted man, and sits enthroned in yonder heavens! That is the great secret. If the veil were rent today, and the great God who holds this world in its orbit, and who upholds all worlds and all things by His power, was to make Himself visible—I say, if you were to see him today, you would see Him like a man in form—like yourselves—in all the person, image, and very form as a man; for Adam was created in the very fashion, image, and likeness of God, and received instruction from, and walked, talked and conversed with Him, as one man talks and communes with another . . . . It is the first principle of the gospel to know for a certainty the character of God, and to know that we may converse with Him as one man converses with another, and that He was once a man like us; yea, that God himself, the Father of us all, dwelt on an earth, the same as Jesus Christ Himself did. ("The King Follett Sermon," *Ensign*, Apr. 1971; this article is a reprint taken from the *Documentary History of the Church*, 6:302–17)

Lorenzo Snow's knowledge from the Prophet Joseph is succinctly expressed in this famous couplet, *"As man is, God once was; as God is, man may become*" (*Teachings of the Presidents of the Church: Lorenzo Snow* [2011], 83; emphasis added).

The Prophet Joseph F. Smith has taught, "We are destined and fore-ordained to become like God, and unless we do become like him we will never be permitted to dwell with him. When we become like him you will find that we will be presented before him in the form in which we were created, male and female" (*Gospel Doctrine: Selections from the Sermons and Writings of Joseph F. Smith*, compiled by John A. Widtsoe [Salt Lake City: *Deseret News*, 1919], 346).

SECOND-CENTURY CHRISTIANS WROTE CONCERNING MAN BECOMING AS THE GODS

Clement of Alexandria (approximately 150–215 AD) had teachings that show he had a belief in the doctrine of men becoming Gods: "'If anyone knows himself he shall know God, and by knowing God he shall be made like unto Him'; and again, 'that man with whom the Logos dwells . . . is made like God and is beautiful . . . that man becomes God, for God so wills it'; and 'the Logos of God became man that from man you might learn how man may become God.' Further, that the true (Christian) Gnostic 'has already become God'" (Samuel Angus, *The Mystery-Religions: A Study in the Religious Background of Early Christianity*, 1975, 88).

Methodius, Bishop of Olympus (d. 311 AD), categorically declared that, "every believer must through participation in Christ be born a Christ," and he also taught assertively that, "He was made man that we might be made God" (Angus, *The Mystery-Religions, 88*).

A plethora of early Christians who wrote concerning the doctrine of deification includes Origen of Alexandria (185–254 AD); Justin Martyr, born in Nablus (100–165 AD); Hippolytus of Rome (170–235 AD); Athanasius of Alexandria (298–373 AD); Augustine. a Bishop of Hippo Regius (354–430 AD); and Jerome, a son of Eusebius (347–420 AD).

OTHER CHRISTIAN WRITERS HAVE DECLARED THAT WE CAN BECOME GODS

C. S. Lewis has stated, "The command *Be ye perfect* is not idealistic gas. Nor is it a command to do the impossible. . . . He [Christ] said (in the Bible) that we were 'gods' and He is going to make good his words. . . . The process will be long and in parts very painful, but that is what we are in for. Nothing less. He meant what He said. . . . Those who put themselves in His hands will become perfect, as He is perfect—perfect in love, wisdom, joy, beauty, and immortality" (*Mere Christianity [New York: HarperSanFrancisco, 2001]*, 205–7).

Yes, the doctrine of deification, or becoming gods, has been taught from the beginning, and the scriptures, prophets, and others have so testified. The question arises, "*How do we become Gods?*"

THE PROCESS OF BECOMING GODS

The process of receiving all that the Father has (see Doctrine and Covenants 84:38) and becoming gods (see Doctrine and Covenants 132:19–20) is by obedience to the principles and ordinances of the gospel, especially those received in the Lord's holy house. The temple, with all its ordinances and covenants, is the only way back to the Father. The Prophet Joseph explains the process of becoming gods: "When you climb up a ladder, you must begin at the bottom, and ascend step by step, until you arrive at the top; and so it is with the principles of the gospel—you must begin with the first, and go on until you learn all the principles of exaltation. But it will be a great while after you have passed through the veil before you will have learned them" (*Teachings of Presidents of the Church: Joseph Smith* [2011], ch. 22).

The Lord has said,

> And this greater priesthood administereth the gospel and holdeth the key of the mysteries of the kingdom, even the key of the knowledge of God. Therefore, in the ordinances thereof, the power of godliness is manifest.

And without the ordinances thereof, and the authority of the priesthood, the power of godliness is not manifest unto men in the flesh; for without this no man can see the face of God, even the Father, and live. (Doctrine and Covenants 84:19–22)

We, through the ordinances and covenants of the temple, better understand the doctrines (the mysteries) and come to a more complete knowledge of God the Father and Christ the Lord. We can become holy as we partake of the power of godliness.

THE POWER OF GODLINESS

The power of godliness is received through the ordinances of the greater priesthood (see Doctrine and Covenants 84:19–22) and is enabled by the Savior's infinite Atonement. The power of godliness helps us possess the qualities of a godlike behavior and countenance that enable us to return to the presence of our Father. If we "deny [ourselves] of all ungodliness, and love God with all [our] might, mind and strength, then is his grace sufficient for [us], that by his grace [we] may be perfect in Christ" (Moroni 10:32). Mormon explains how part of this power can be ours: "Pray unto the Father with all the energy of heart, that ye may be filled with this love, which he hath bestowed upon all who are true followers of his Son, Jesus Christ; that ye may become the sons of God; that when he shall appear we shall be like him, for we shall see him as he is; that we may have this hope; that we may be purified even as he is pure" (Moroni 7:48). This priesthood power and blessing were exactly what the churches in the days of the Prophet Joseph Smith were lacking: "They draw near to me with their lips, but their hearts are far from me, they teach for doctrines the

> *The power of godliness is received through the ordinances of the greater priesthood.*

commandments of men, having a form of godliness, but they deny the power thereof" (Joseph Smith—History 1:19).

As part of the perfection process, the ordinances of the temple literally empower us to become godly. Godliness is all about becoming like God, which is the essence and purpose of the temple. This is why Moroni speaks of this doctrine as he closes the Book of Mormon (see Moroni 10:32–33). We become perfected as we deny every form of ungodliness and become godly; then His grace is sufficient for us.

We can receive the fullness of the Holy Ghost as we worship in the temple. "And that all people who shall enter upon the threshold of the Lord's house may feel thy power, and feel constrained to acknowledge . . . that it is thy house, . . . that they may grow up in thee, and receive a fulness of the Holy Ghost" (Doctrine and Covenants 109:13–15). With godliness, we will have "a godly walk and conversation, . . . that there may be works and faith agreeable to the holy scriptures—walking in holiness before the Lord" (Doctrine and Covenants 20:69). The power of godliness is a gift of grace; it comes to us individually as we prepare ourselves to receive it, through the ordinances of the priesthood in the temple.

All these truths come by revelation. Elder John A. Widtsoe taught, "The endowment is so richly symbolic. . . . It is so packed full of revelations to those who exercise their strength to seek and see, that no human words can explain or make clear the possibilities that reside in the temple service. The endowment which was given by revelation can best be understood by revelation" ("Symbolism in the Temples," quoted in "Why Symbols?" *Ensign* or *Liahona*, Feb. 2007).

The Prophet Joseph counseled us to "search deeper and deeper into the mysteries of Godliness" (*Teachings of Presidents of the Church: Joseph Smith* [2011], ch. 8). Surely this requires us to come to the house of the Lord to worship and receive revelation, which is the key to understanding.

Godliness is to serve as the Lord would serve and do as He would do and say the things that He would say. Godliness is holiness, righteousness, and saintliness; it is taking upon oneself the divine nature of Christ.

Surely the knowledge of God and the power of godliness were part of the underlying theme of Peter's epistle when he said, "Grace and peace be multiplied unto you through the knowledge of God, and of Jesus our Lord, according as his divine power hath given unto us all things that pertain unto life and godliness, through the knowledge of him that hath called us to glory and virtue: whereby are given unto us exceeding great and precious promises: that by these ye might be partakers of the divine nature, having escaped the corruption that is in the world through lust" (2 Peter 1:2–4). Then Peter taught the process for possessing the pure love of Christ: "And beside this, giving all diligence, add to your faith virtue; and to virtue knowledge; and to knowledge temperance; and to temperance patience; and to patience godliness; and to godliness brotherly kindness; and to brotherly kindness charity" (2 Peter 1:5–7), following which Peter wanted us to do these things "to make [our] calling and election sure" (2 Peter 1:10).

CALLING AND ELECTION MADE SURE—THE MORE SURE WORD OF PROPHECY

One of the least talked about and most misunderstood doctrines of the gospel of Jesus Christ is that of making our calling and election sure. Our *calling* is your name, i.e., a son or daughter of God, a divine child of God, destined through our faithfulness to become like our Heavenly Parents. We have been called to serve. It is our holy calling to receive all that the Father has as we receive our Savior and His prophets . . . to become like Him through our faithfulness (see Doctrine and Covenants 84:38; 3 Nephi 12:48). Our *election* refers to being selected according to our worthiness and righteousness to receive all that the Father has, and thus the Holy Spirit of Promise seals us up unto eternal life. Then our calling and election are made sure.

Our calling and election being made sure is about being worthy to come back into the presence of the Father and the Son. It is about being qualified to be made perfect and complete.

All the attributes mentioned by Peter (see 2 Peter 1:5–7) and in Doctrine and Covenants 4:6 (faith, virtue, knowledge, temperance, patience, brotherly kindness, godliness, charity, humility, diligence) are part of the building blocks to receive and possess charity, or the pure love of Christ.

Faith. Faith is to have belief and hope in Jesus Christ and the truth; it is the moving cause of all action and the power to do all things.

Virtue. Virtue is the power that stems from righteousness.

Gospel knowledge. We are to "live by every word that proceedeth forth from the mouth of God" (Doctrine and Covenants 84:44); therefore, we must treasure up the word of God in the scriptures and from the prophets.

Temperance. Temperance reflects moderation and self-control.

Patience. Being patient connotes the capacity of enduring well without murmuring, being calm and without haste, practicing long-suffering, being slow to anger, being constant, and persevering. It is integrally connected to charity

Brotherly kindness. Loving-kindness is compassion and caring for others, thus fulfilling the great commandment of love.

Godliness. Godliness is a state of holiness, piety, and meekness. We live the laws of God. We seek to become like Him. We deny ourselves of all ungodliness—worldliness, selfishness, etc.—we become more Christlike (see Moroni 7:48) and full of charity.

Humility. Humility is knowing our relationship with God and our dependence upon Him. We will then obtain the fruits of humility—submissiveness, easily entreated, and teachable so that we can be an instrument in the hands of the Lord Jesus Christ.

Diligence. Diligence is the careful and constant effort as we work with all our heart, might, mind, and strength.

The Prophet Joseph has exhorted us to make our calling and election sure. He said, "I am going on in my progress for eternal life," and then he implores us, "Oh! I beseech you to go forward, go forward and make your calling and your election sure; and if any man preach any other Gospel than that which I have preached, he shall be cursed; and some of you who now hear me shall see it, and know that I testify the truth concerning them" (B. H. Roberts, *History of the Church*, 7 vols. [Salt Lake City: *Deseret News*, 1902], 6:365).

We recognize that the gift of eternal life is fulfilled following mortality, but the knowledge of that precious gift can give us peace and can be received here on earth. "But learn that he who doeth the works of righteousness shall receive his reward, even peace in this world, and eternal life in the world to come" (Doctrine and Covenants 59:23). Heavenly Father's work is our immortality and eternal life—even eternal lives. His desire is that we might live a life like Him.

> They shall pass by the angels, and the gods, which are set there, to their exaltation and glory in all things, as hath been sealed upon their heads, which glory shall be a fulness and a continuation of the seeds forever and ever. Then shall they be gods, because they have no end; therefore shall they be from everlasting to everlasting, because they continue; then shall they be above all, because all things are subject unto them. Then shall they be gods, because they have all power, and the angels are subject unto them. (Doctrine and Covenants 132:19–20)

Thus, the Prophet Joseph said, "You have got to learn how to be gods yourselves, and to be kings and priests to God" (*Teachings of Presidents of the Church: Joseph Smith* [2011], ch. 18).

The promise of eternal life is knowing that your calling and election are sure. "The more sure word of prophecy means a man's knowing that he is sealed up unto eternal life, by revelation and the spirit of prophecy, through the power of the Holy Priesthood" (Doctrine and Covenants 131:5).

Elder Bruce R. McConkie has taught,

> To have one's calling and election made sure is to be sealed up unto eternal life; it is to have the unconditional

guarantee of exaltation in the highest heaven of the
celestial world; it is to receive the assurance of godhood;
it is, in effect, to have the day of judgment advanced,
so that an inheritance of all the glory and honor of the
Father's kingdom is assured prior to the day when the
faithful actually enter into the divine presence to sit
with Christ in his throne, even as he is 'set down' with
his 'Father in his throne' (Revelation 3:21). (*Doctrinal
New Testament Commentary*, 3 vols. [Salt Lake City:
Bookcraft, 1973], 3:330–31)

Examples of these blessings are found in the scriptures:

To Alma the Lord said, "Thou art my servant; and I covenant with
thee that thou shalt have eternal life" (Mosiah 26:20).

To Joseph Smith the Lord said, "For I am the Lord thy God, and
will be with thee [Joseph] even unto the end of the world, and through
all eternity; for verily I seal upon you your exaltation, and prepare a
throne for you in the kingdom of my Father, with Abraham your father"
(Doctrine and Covenants 132:49).

Surely our hearts yearn to become godly and full of charity, which
never faileth. We would do well to ask ourselves a few questions regarding
the power necessary to become godly. What can we do to bring the
sanctifying power of the priesthood into our lives? How will our "lists
of life" take on a new dimension as a result of our seeking to have our
calling and election made sure? How can we go about doing good? How
will we learn to better please God and deny ourselves of all ungodliness?

As I recently pondered these questions again, I realized that the answer
to these questions is the simple phrase, "Do as Jesus would do." To deny
myself of all ungodliness, I must take up my cross—my trials and tribulations. I must be willing to give my all for the kingdom of God, that
the children of God may be nourished by the good word of God. Christ
gave His all that we might live. We give our all that we might invite all to

Surely our hearts yearn to become godly and full of charity.

come unto Christ and live with God in everlasting happiness.

ETERNAL MARRIAGE—THE ULTIMATE TEMPLE ORDINANCE

The Lord has said, "Behold, I will send you Elijah the prophet before the coming of the great and dreadful day of the Lord: and he shall turn the heart of the fathers to the children, and the heart of the children to their fathers, *lest I come and smite the earth with a curse*" (Malachi 4:5–6; emphasis added). And He again reminds us, "I will reveal unto you the Priesthood, by the hand of Elijah the prophet, before the coming of the great and dreadful day of the Lord. And he shall plant in the hearts of the children the promises made to the fathers, and the hearts of the children shall turn to their fathers. *If it were not so, the whole earth would be utterly wasted at his coming*" (Doctrine and Covenants 2:1–3; emphasis added). And in the Doctrine and Covenants, section 138, verses 47–48, we read: "The Prophet Elijah was to plant in the hearts of the children the promises made to their fathers, foreshadowing the great work to be done in the temples of the Lord in the dispensation of the fulness of times, for the redemption of the dead, and the sealing of the children to their parents, lest the whole earth be smitten with a curse and utterly wasted at his coming." We have been clearly and repeatedly taught that the whole earth would be wasted and cursed, and the plan of God not fulfilled, without the great sealing power of the priesthood as it has been restored in its fullness in these latter days. The restoration of all things includes the sealing power that eternally binds the members of the family of God into eternal families.

The life-exalting ordinances in the temple are all about families. It naturally follows that the Church is about families as well, for they are the basic unit of the Church, and we are all members of a family. Families really are forever. The Family Proclamation teaches this about members of families: "Each is a beloved spirit son or daughter of heavenly parents, and, as such, each has a divine nature and destiny" ("The Family: A Proclamation to the World," *Ensign* or *Liahona*, Nov. 2010, 129).

Questions to Ponder

- What is my plan to take upon the divine nature of Christ?

- What is one way the power of godliness is manifest in my life?

Epilogue

CHRIST'S INVITATION TO US—
"COME UNTO ME," "COME FOLLOW ME"

THE LORD HAS PLEADED, "COME unto me" and "Come follow me." Each scripture has a special blessing for our coming to and following the Lord. Every aspect of the Lord's life leading up to His ultimate sacrifice and Atonement was lived with a purpose to draw us to Him. "And my Father sent me that I might be lifted up upon the cross; *and after that I had been lifted up upon the cross, that I might draw all men unto me*" (3 Nephi 27:14; emphasis added). Note each blessing in the following scriptures.

> Now this is the commandment: Repent, all ye ends of the earth, and *come unto me* and be baptized in my name, that ye may be sanctified by the reception of the Holy Ghost, that ye may stand spotless before me at the last day. (3 Nephi 27:20; emphasis added; see also 3 Nephi 30:2; Mormon 3:2; Ether 4:18; Moroni 7:34)

Each commandment is given in love by our Savior. All commandments come with promised blessings. The commandment given in this verse is the doctrine of Christ. To be received of Christ we must have faith unto repentance, be baptized in His name, and be sanctified by the

Each commandment is given in love by our Savior.

reception of the Holy Ghost . . . and then we will receive the promised blessing to stand spotless before the Lord at the last day.

> Therefore, whoso repenteth and *cometh unto me* as a little child, him will I receive, for of such is the kingdom of God. Behold, for such I have laid down my life, and have taken it up again; therefore repent, and *come unto me* ye ends of the earth, and be saved. (3 Nephi 9:22; emphasis added)

When we repent and come unto the Lord as a little child, He will receive us into His kingdom because we are "submissive, meek, humble, patient, full of love, willing to submit to all things" (Mosiah 3:19).

> And behold, I have given you the law and the commandments of my Father, that ye shall believe in me, and that ye shall repent of your sins, and *come unto me* with a broken heart and a contrite spirit. Behold, ye have the commandments before you, and the law is fulfilled. (3 Nephi 12:19; emphasis added)

When we come unto the Lord, we are repentant, having godly sorrow for our sins, which makes us worthy of being baptized and partaking of the sacrament because our sacrificial offering is a "broken heart and contrite spirit."

> Therefore, if ye shall *come unto me*, or shall desire to come unto me, and rememberest that thy brother hath aught against thee—go thy way unto thy brother, and first be

reconciled to thy brother, *and then come unto me* with full
purpose of heart, and I will receive you. (3 Nephi 12:23–
24; emphasis added)

When we come unto the Lord, it is important to be reconciled to
others where there have been some misgivings. We will have no divided
loyalties and no spiritually debilitating distractions. We come to Him
with a full purpose of heart so He will receive us.

Yea, verily I say unto you, if ye will *come unto me* ye
shall have eternal life. Behold, mine arm of mercy is
extended towards you, and whosoever will come, him
will I receive; and blessed are those who *come unto me.*
Behold, I am Jesus Christ the Son of God. I created the
heavens and the earth, and all things that in them are.
I was with the Father from the beginning. I am in the
Father, and the Father in me; and in me hath the Father
glorified his name. (3 Nephi 9:14–15; emphasis added)

The Son of God—the Creator of heaven and earth, the Savior of all
mankind—is waiting to receive all worthy followers and promises us the
blessing of eternal life. When we come unto the Lord with full purpose
of heart, He will receive us, and we shall have eternal life.

And ye see that I have commanded that none of you
should go away, but rather have commanded that ye
should *come unto me,* that ye might feel and see; even so
shall ye do unto the world; and whosoever breaketh this
commandment suffereth himself to be led into tempta-
tion. (3 Nephi 18:25; emphasis added)

After the Nephite saints came to see the Savior and to feel His wounds,
they were commanded by Him to go to all the world and testify of these
things. And when we come to Christ, we are duty bound to testify of Him

"and to stand as witnesses of God at all times and in all things, and in all places that [we] may be in, even until death, that [we] may be redeemed of God, and be numbered with those of the first resurrection, that [we] may have eternal life" (Mosiah 18:9).

> Nevertheless, ye shall not cast him out of your synagogues, or your places of worship, for unto such shall ye continue to minister; for ye know not but what they will return and repent, and *come unto me* with full purpose of heart, and I shall heal them; and ye shall be the means of bringing salvation unto them. (3 Nephi 18:32; emphasis added)

The Savior here admonishes us to always be patient with those who are struggling and to seek to help them to come unto Christ, for He is mighty to save. As we assist others to come unto Christ, our joy will be full because their souls are so precious. "Remember the worth of souls is great in the sight of God. . . . And how great is his joy in the soul that repenteth. . . . And if it so be that you should labor all your days in crying repentance unto this people, and bring save it be one soul unto me, how great shall be your joy with him in the kingdom of my Father" (see Doctrine and Covenants 18:10–16)!

> And I soon go to the place of my rest, which is with my Redeemer; for I know that in him I shall rest. And I rejoice in the day when my mortal shall put on immortality, and shall stand before him; then shall I see his face with pleasure, and he will say unto me: *Come unto me*, ye blessed, there is a place prepared for you in the mansions of my Father. (Enos 1:27; emphasis added)

Note that this verse at the close of the book of Enos has a completely different connotation regarding "come unto me." Enos has lived a faithful life and expresses his joy as he anticipates coming into the presence of the Son of God. With faith and confidence, he mentions what the Lord will say unto him: "*Come unto me, ye blessed, there is a place prepared for you in the mansions of my Father. Amen.*" The Lord is inviting him to come into the glory of God. When we come to the end of our mortal sojourn and stand before the Lord, having been faithful and diligent in keeping the commandments and enduring to the end, we too can enter into His eternal rest.

> I say unto you, can you imagine to yourselves that ye hear the voice of the Lord, saying unto you, in that day: *Come unto me* ye blessed, for behold, your works have been the works of righteousness upon the face of the earth. (Alma 5:16; emphasis added)

Alma asks us to imagine that at the end of our days we hear the voice of the Lord inviting us to come unto Him, into His presence, because our works have been the works of righteousness. Can we imagine our joy and gratitude at that great and glorious day? I love to envision that homecoming back into the presence of the Father and the Son, "encircled about eternally in the arms of [Their] love" (2 Nephi 1:15).

The Lord has made clear that we are to come unto Him and receive Him by receiving the ordinances and principles of the gospel of Jesus Christ. Coming unto the Lord requires us to take action. When we receive Him, then He will receive us. The Lord said, "For he that receiveth my servants receiveth me; and he that receiveth me receiveth my Father; and he that receiveth my Father receiveth my Father's kingdom; therefore all that my Father hath shall be given unto him. And this is according to the oath and covenant which belongeth to the priesthood" (Doctrine and Covenants 84:36–39). This refers to the highest ordinances received in the temple.

The Lord reminds us, "Draw near unto me and I will draw near unto you; seek me diligently and ye shall find me; ask, and ye shall receive; knock, and it shall be opened unto you" (Doctrine and Covenants 88:63). When we come close to the Lord, we literally become empowered by Him. The Lord described this when He said, "And whoso receiveth you, there I will be also, for I will go before your face. I will be on your right hand and on your left, and my Spirit shall be in your hearts, and mine angels round about you, to bear you up" (Doctrine and Covenants 84:88). Matthew records, "Come unto me, all ye that labour and are heavy laden, and I will give you rest. Take my yoke upon you, and learn of me; for I am meek and lowly in heart: and ye shall find rest unto your souls. For my yoke is easy, and my burden is light" (Matthew 11:28–30). This invitation comes with an eternal promise. The Lord's yoke refers to humbly doing His will and allowing Him to guide and direct us in all things and to succor us as well (see Alma 7:11–12). The Lord "shall give [us] rest" (2 Nephi 24:3) for our souls. Rest from all our pains and sufferings. Alma taught, "The spirits of those who are righteous are received into a state of happiness, which is called paradise, a state of rest, a state of peace, where they shall rest from all their troubles and from all care, and sorrow" (Alma 40:12).

The invitation to come unto Christ is the initial step toward happiness and eternal life.

The Lord has also exhorted us, "Come, follow me."

> And when he had called the people unto him with his disciples also, he said unto them, Whosoever will come after me, let him *deny himself, and take up his cross, and follow me.* (Mark 8:34; see also Matthew 16:24; Luke 9:23; emphasis added)

The Prophet Joseph translated the foregoing passage as follows: "Then said Jesus unto his disciples, If any man will come after me, let him deny himself, and take up his cross, and follow me. *And now for a man to take up his cross, is to deny himself all ungodliness, and every worldly lust, and keep my commandments*" (Joseph Smith Translation, Matthew 16:24 [see also Matthew 16:24, footnote *d*]; emphasis added). Then in an expanded translation we read, "Break not my commandments for to save your lives; for whosoever will save his life in this world, shall lose it in the world to come. And whosoever will lose his life in this world, for my sake, shall find it in the world to come" (Joseph Smith Translation, Matthew 16:27–29). When we follow Christ, we follow His example in all things. Worry not, for He will provide a way to keep His commandments (see 1 Nephi 3:7), give us the strength to keep the commandments (see Alma 26:11–12), and if we are humble and exercise faith in Him, He will make weak things become strong (see Ether 12:27).

> *When we come close to the Lord, we literally become empowered by Him.*

> And he saith unto them, *Follow me*, and I will make you fishers of men. And they straightway left their nets, and followed him. (Matthew 4:19–20; emphasis added)

With the invitation to follow Him, the Lord makes a proclamation to His newfound disciples. He will make them fishers of men. Elder James E. Talmage explains this symbolism beautifully: "The contrast thus presented between their former vocation and their new calling is strikingly forceful. Theretofore they had caught fish, and the fate of the fish was death; thereafter they were to draw [catch] men—to a life eternal" (*Jesus the Christ* [Salt Lake City: The Church of Jesus Christ of Latter-day Saints, 1981], 198–99). They, and we, will become instruments in the Lord's hands to bring souls unto Him (see Alma 29:9–10; Doctrine and Covenants 15:6). This was Alma's glory and joy, and it will be ours too as we bring souls to Christ (see Doctrine and Covenants 18:10–16).

> Jesus said unto him, If thou wilt be perfect, go and sell that thou hast, and give to the poor, and thou shalt have

treasure in heaven: and *come and follow me.* (Matthew 19:21; emphasis added)

Then Jesus beholding him loved him, and said unto him, One thing thou lackest: go thy way, sell whatsoever thou hast, and give to the poor, and thou shalt have treasure in heaven: *and come, take up the cross, and follow me.* (Mark 10:21; emphasis added; see also Luke 18:22)

These scriptures in the synoptic gospels of Matthew, Mark, and Luke teach a difficult doctrine to assimilate. This young man came to the Lord with a question concerning eternal life and what he needed to do to qualify for it. I love Mark's account, for the first words Mark records are, "Then Jesus beholding him loved him." The Lord loved him! Apparently, the young man was doing everything he should as he admitted to keeping the commandments since his youth, yet he is concerned and the Lord intimates that he lacketh "one thing." The question is, "Where are your treasures?" The Savior's advice to sell everything is symbolic in that the Lord is asking for complete devotion . . . and then the Lord said, "Come follow me" and your treasures will be in heaven. We have been given the same choice to follow Him and walk in His ways, to serve others and enjoy the blessings of exaltation. The young man in this case was grieved because he could not leave his worldly treasures, and he went away sorrowing. Following this incident, the Lord taught concerning the rich and the difficulty they have in entering the kingdom of heaven (see Matthew 19:22–24) because their hearts are set on the things of this world. The burning questions to us are, "Where are our treasures?" "What are our values?" "What sins are we holding onto that give us worldly pleasures?" This is *not* about selling all and being penniless. It *is* about serving with all our heart, might, mind, and strength for the kingdom of God and the building up of Zion. This question is about a consecrated life.

When we make the Lord our Shepherd, we become His flock and we know His voice and we follow Him (see John 10:27). When we choose to serve the Lord, He reminds us, "If any man serve me, let him follow me; and where I am, there shall also my servant be: if any man serve me, him will my Father honour" (John 12:26). Blessings follow the servants of the Lord. Nephi explains, "And now, my beloved brethren, I know by this that unless a man shall endure to the end, in following the example of the Son of the living God, he cannot be saved" (2 Nephi 31:16).

The commandment to follow Christ is the sure and safe pathway to happiness and eternal life.

The Lord reminds His true disciples and followers, "Learn of me, and listen to my words; walk in the meekness of my Spirit, and you shall have peace in me" (Doctrine and Covenants 19:23)—a wondrous promise from the Prince of Peace.

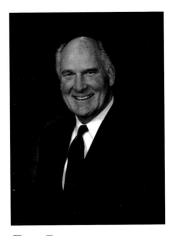

About the Author

ED J. PINEGAR IS THE author of more than sixty nonfiction books, audio-books, and talks.

He has had the opportunity to teach at Brigham Young University, the Orem Institute of Religion, the Provo MTC, various seminaries, and BYU Education Week. He has been blessed with the opportunity to serve in many positions of leadership within The Church of Jesus Christ of Latter-day Saints, most recently serving as the Manti Temple president.

He and his wife, Pat, are the parents of eight, grandparents of thirty-eight, and great-grandparents of twenty-five. Ed and his wife live in Orem, Utah.